FIVE-MINUTE BIBLE CRAFTS

by
Susan J. Stegenga

illustrated by Darcy Tom

Cover by Kathryn R. Marlin

Copyright © 1994, Shining Star Publications

ISBN No. 1-56417-004-7

Standardized Subject Code TA ac

Printing No. 987

Shining Star
A Division of Frank Schaffer Publications, Inc.
23740 Hawthorne Boulevard, Torrance, CA 90505-5927

Unless otherwise indicated, the New International Version of the Bible was used in preparing the activities in this book.

Table of Contents

SS3826

Dedication

In loving memory of my grandparents, Dr. Thies and Aletta DeYoung and Rev. Miner and Dureth Stegenga–they passed on the enduring values of faith, family, education, and creativity. They passed on these values to my parents, who in turn shared this inheritance with me.

This book is evidence of my family's continuing influence in my life. I'm grateful to the Lord for this precious inheritance.

To the Teacher/Parent

Youngsters today are growing up in a hectic era of television and computers. Children become accustomed to quick results and immediate feedback. Rather than denying this reality, we need to adjust our teaching and parenting styles to meet the needs of today's children.

Of course, there are times when long-term, detailed projects are helpful for building skills such as patience and concentration. There are many other occasions when you have only a few minutes available, and want to use those moments wisely. If you're in a classroom setting, those minutes might be when students first arrive or shortly before they leave. These projects might also be used as rewards or treats when students finish other assignments. If you're a parent, these projects make wonderful quiet-time activities that you and your child can do together. Many of the projects may also be used as gifts for holidays or celebrations such as Mother's Day, Father's Day, or Christmas.

The instructional steps provided for the child generally can be completed in three to five minutes. Remember, though, that every child is different. What takes one several minutes to finish can take another twice as long. Keep in mind the specific abilities and age level of each child as you plan activities.

Some of the activities are intended to be group projects in which each individual child spends a few minutes participating.

Other project pages include several ideas or options. Choose only what is appropriate for the time you have available. For example, some pages provide several different patterns. If you have only a few minutes, each child may use one pattern. Or, if time allows, a child may choose to use several different patterns.

Allow extra time for adult preparation such as making copies, cutting out patterns, or mixing up a batch of clay. If you have enough time, an older child may help with preparation.

Any steps involving potentially dangerous equipment such as a hot iron or sharp hobby knife need to be done by an adult or with adult supervision, depending on the child's age. An eleven-year-old may be able to iron a T-shirt with supervision, while it would be unsafe for a five-year-old. Generally, only an adult should use a hobby knife.

There may also be some adult follow-up required, such as baking, to complete a project. Additional time may be needed for a project to air-dry after the child makes it.

Be flexible as you use these ideas. Choose projects according to the time you have available and each child's needs.

Armor of God Costume
Breastplate of Righteousness

Materials

Large plain brown paper grocery bag
Scissors
Crayons or markers

Instructions

1. Turn bag upside down. Cut a slit down the front, center of the bag.
2. Cut a hole for the neck.
3. With an adult's help, cut out armholes on the sides of the bag.
4. Turn the bag around so the slit is in the back, lay it flat, and color and decorate the front. Write the word "Righteousness" on the front (see Ephesians 6:10-17). Draw the "Belt of Truth" on the bag.
5. Open the bag and put your head and arms through the holes. Wear the costume with the slit in back.

Other Idea

1. Use these ideas to make other Bible costumes for plays, skits, etc. For example, wear this armor to be a Roman soldier in an Easter play.

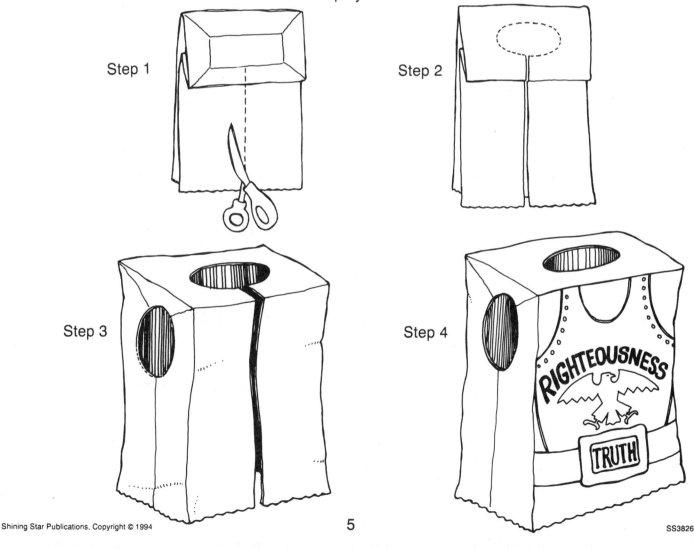

Step 1   Step 2   Step 3   Step 4

Armor of God Costume
Helmet of Salvation

Materials
Small plain brown paper grocery bag
Scissors
Crayons or markers

Instructions
1. Turn paper bag upside down.
2. Cut an opening in the front of the bag as shown.
3. Draw a decorative design and write the word "Salvation" on the bag.
4. Pull the bag open and put it on your head with the opening in front for your face.
5. Wear the helmet as part of the Armor of God costume.

Armor of God Costume
Sword and Shield

Materials
Shield pattern (page 8)
Heavy paper or cardboard
Crayons or markers
Scissors
Glue
Stapler and staples or clear tape
Long cardboard tube
Scraps of heavy paper or cardboard
Ruler

Adult Preparation
1. Copy the shield on page 8 on heavy paper or mount it on cardboard.

Instructions
1. Color the shield.
2. If the shield is on lightweight paper, glue it to cardboard and cut around the edges.
3. Cut a strip of heavy paper or cardboard 7" x 2" for the shield's handle.
4. Staple or tape the ends of the strip to the back of the shield.
5. To make the sword, cut a long strip of cardboard into the shape of a sword, or start with a long cardboard tube. Staple or tape another strip of cardboard to the sword for a handle. Snip the other end of the sword on an angle to make the point.

Other Ideas
1. Decorate the shield and sword with foil scraps, glitter or glitter glue, metallic crayons, or glow-in-the-dark paints or pens.
2. Remember that these items are not meant to be used to fight with other people, but to remind you to fight evil with God's Word, the Bible.

 SS3826

Ephesians 6:16

The Shield
of
FAITH
✝

SS3826

Royal Crown

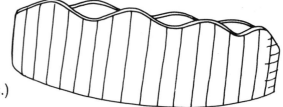

Materials
Colored corrugated cardboard (used for bulletin board borders; can be purchased in inexpensive rolls at teachers' supply or craft stores)
Scissors
Glue
Stapler and staples
Craft glue
Decorative trims (sequins, glitter glue, shiny beads, etc.)

Adult Preparation
1. Hold a strip of corrugated cardboard around child's head to measure size needed.
2. Cut cardboard strip to fit child's head, allowing a little extra at the ends for overlap.

Instructions
1. Decorate the outside of the cardboard to look like a crown.
2. Ask an adult to help you overlap the back edges slightly, then staple the edges to make a crown.
3. Wear the crown to act out Bible stories of Bible characters such as King David or Queen Esther.

Other Ideas
1. Use bobby pins or hair clips to keep the crown on your head while wearing it.
2. Make a miniature crown for a puppet or a doll. Use the miniature figure to act out a Bible story.

SS3826

Bible-Time Buildings

Materials
Medium and small boxes (shoe boxes, gift boxes, etc.)
Markers or crayons
Scissors
Clear tape

Instructions
1. Remove lids from boxes.
2. Turn boxes upside down.
3. Draw windows and doors on the sides of the boxes.
4. With an adult's help, cut out openings for the windows and doors, or leave a vertical side uncut on each door and window so it will open and close.
5. Tape box lids of different sizes together to make steps leading to the roof of a building.
6. Make buildings such as homes, temples, and palaces. Place buildings on a table to create a Bible-time scene. Use the scene to tell a Bible story.

Other Ideas
1. Several children may work together to create a scene. If each child makes one building to contribute to the scene, it will be done in a few minutes.
2. Use the ideas shown on the following pages to make trees, miniature animals, and people to add to the scene.

Cardboard Tube Palm Trees

Materials

Cardboard tubes (bathroom tubes or paper towel tubes)
Palm branch pattern (bottom of this page)
Green crayon and white paper (or green construction paper scraps)
Scissors
Pencil
Clear tape

Adult Preparation

1. Copy the palm branch pattern below.
2. Cut out the palm branch and trace it on green or white paper. Trace several branches for each tree.

Instructions

1. Color the branches green if on white paper.
2. Cut out branches.
3. Turn each cardboard tube upright and cut to desired tree trunk height.
4. Tape the stems of several branches to the top of each tube.
5. Use palm trees to decorate a Bible-time scene.

Other Ideas

1. For a Bible-time scene, use the palm trees with other items such as Bible-time buildings (page 10) and animals and people (pages 12-13).
2. Place the scene on a tabletop or in a box of sand to make a desert scene.
3. Use the palm-branch pattern to make miniature palm leaves to act out the Palm Sunday story. Make palm branches to be held by paper doll or cardboard tube figures (pages 14-16 and pages 23-24).

SS3826

Cotton Ball Lambs

Materials

Cotton balls (or large and small white pom-poms)
Decorative trims (felt scraps, tiny plastic wiggle eyes, tiny pink pom-poms, etc.)
Craft glue
Scissors

Instructions

1. Choose large ball of cotton or a pom-pom to use as the lamb's body.
2. Use another smaller ball of cotton or pom-pom for the head. Glue the smaller ball to the larger ball.
3. Cut bits of felt and glue them on the head and body for details such as ears. Glue tiny eyes to the head. Glue small pom-poms on lamb for nose, feet, tail, etc.
4. Use lambs in a miniature Bible-time scene or to act out stories involving shepherds and sheep such as the Christmas story.

SS3826

Bible-Time Clothespin Dolls

Materials

Nonclamp-type clothespins (one for each doll)
Fabric scraps
Craft glue
Yarn scraps
Scissors
Chenille stems (pipe cleaners)
Fine-line permanent markers
Lump of molding clay or play dough

Instructions

1. To make the doll's arms, cut a piece of chenille stem and wrap it around the clothespin. Bend back the ends of the wire to make the doll's hands.
2. Cut out a small rectangle from fabric for the doll's robe. Cut a small neck hole in the middle. Ask an adult to help you. Slip the doll's head through the neck hole.
3. Cut a piece of yarn and tie it around the doll's waist for a belt.
4. Cut a scrap of fabric for a headpiece. Glue it to the head. Cut and tie a piece of yarn around the head, or glue bits of yarn to the head for the hair.
5. Use a marker to draw eyes, mouth, and nose.
6. Place doll in a lump of clay to make it stand up.
7. Bend another piece of chenille stem and attach it to the doll's hand for a shepherd's staff.

Other Ideas

1. Use dolls as part of a tabletop Bible scene using buildings (page 10), palm trees (page 11), and lambs (page 12).
2. Use dolls with lambs to act out Bible-time scenes involving shepherds.

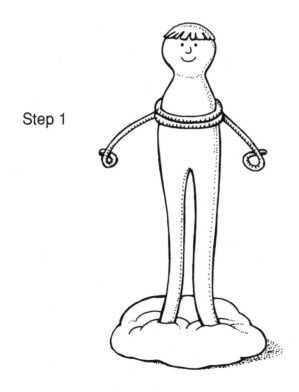

Step 1

Steps 2-7

Bible-Time Paper-Doll Family

Materials
Paper-doll patterns (pages 15-16)
Heavy paper or lightweight cardboard
Scissors
Crayons, colored pencils, or markers
Decorative trims (fabric scraps, yarn scraps, paper scraps, tiny wiggle eyes, etc.)
Glue

Adult Preparation
1. Copy the paper-doll figures on pages 15-16 on heavy paper. (Since each doll will take several minutes to make, plan to have each child make only one doll per session.)
2. If using lightweight paper for the copies, allow extra time for the child to glue figures on cardboard to make them sturdier. (You may choose to do this in advance.)

Instructions
1. Cut the dolls and their stands on the dark outlines.
2. If necessary, glue patterns to cardboard backing and trim edges. If you are not planning to make paper-doll clothing, color and apply decorative trims directly on the dolls.
3. Cut dark vertical lines to make a slit on each doll and doll's stand. Fit the doll in the stand to make the doll stand up.
4. If you plan to make paper-doll clothing (see page 17), ask an adult to make slits as indicated by small dark lines on paper dolls. (The clothing tabs will fit in these slits.)
5. The tabs on the paper-doll baby will fit in the slits on the woman's shoulders so she can hold the baby. Fold back the tabs after inserting them into slits.
6. Use the paper dolls to act out Bible stories, such as baby Moses' or Jesus' birth.

Other Idea
1. To protect paper dolls and make them more durable, cover them with clear adhesive plastic.

Bible-Time Paper Dolls

Man

Woman

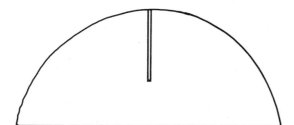

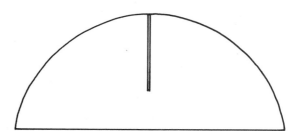

15

SS3826

Bible-Time Paper Dolls

Boy

Girl

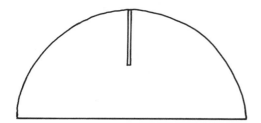

Baby

SS3826

Paper-Doll Clothing

Materials
Sturdy paper
Paper-doll clothing patterns (page 18)
Paper dolls (see pages 14-16)
Crayons, colored pencils, or markers
Decorative trims (fabric scraps, glitter or glitter glue, tiny beads, metallic rickrack, etc.)
Scissors
Glue

Adult Preparation
1. Copy paper-doll clothing patterns on page 18 on sturdy paper.

Instructions
1. Cut out an outfit for each doll.
2. Decorate clothing by coloring or gluing on trims.
3. Insert tabs into slits on each paper doll to dress it. Fold back the tabs behind the doll.
4. Use the dolls to act out Bible stories involving royalty, such as King David and Queen Esther.

Other Ideas
1. Use pattern shapes to make other clothes for your doll's wardrobe.
2. Rather than using the paper tabs to attach clothing to dolls, cut off the tabs and add Velcro™ dots to the clothing and each doll. (Use sturdy paper for clothing so the clothing doesn't rip when removing it, or cover clothing with clear adhesive plastic.)

Paper-Doll Clothing

King's Crown

Queen's Crown

King's Robe

Queen's Robe

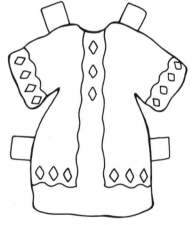

Prince's Robe

Princess' Dress

SS3826

Clothespin Bible-Time Animals

Materials

Animal patterns (pages 20-21)
Heavyweight paper (or lightweight paper and cardboard)
Crayons, colored pencils, or markers
Scissors
Glue
Wooden clamp-type clothespins (two for each animal)

Adult Preparation

1. Make copies of animal patterns, pages 20-21, on heavy paper. (Keep in mind that each animal will take several minutes to make, so you may want to have each child make only one animal per session.)
2. If you use lightweight paper for the copies, allow extra time for children to glue figures to cardboard to make them sturdier. (Or you may do this in advance.)

Instructions

1. Cut out an animal.
2. Cut off the paper legs of each animal. (The animals with their legs will be used for another project on page 22.)
3. Color each animal.
4. Clamp two clothespins to each animal to be its "legs" so it will stand up. (Slant the clothespins slightly so animals won't fall over.)
5. Use the animals as part of a Bible-time scene or to act out specific Bible stories.

Other Idea

1. Glue on decorative trims such as tiny plastic wiggle eyes, yarn on tails, felt scraps, or cotton as wool on lamb.

Bible-Time Animal Pattern

Camel

SS3826

Bible-Time Animal Patterns

Sheep

Donkey

SS3826

Flannelgraph Board

Materials
Flat sheet of cardboard (such as a pizza box lid)
Flannel to fit the cardboard
Scissors
Glue
Bible-time figures (people patterns on pages 15-16 and animals on pages 20-21)
Crayons or markers
Scraps of felt or sandpaper

Adult Preparation
1. Copy people and animal patterns on pages 15-16 and 20-21. You may reduce or enlarge the patterns as you wish.
2. Trim cardboard as needed.

Instructions
1. Color the people and animal figures.
2. Cut out the figures.
3. Cut out small squares of felt or sandpaper and glue them to the backs of the figures.
4. Glue soft flannel to the cardboard or inside the box lid. (If necessary, ask an adult to help you cut the flannel.)
5. Stick the figures onto the flannel to tell a Bible story.

Other Ideas
1. An adult may make the flannel board ahead of time. Each child may make one figure to put on the board for telling a story.
2. Light-blue flannel works well as a background color.
3. Use permanent markers to draw background pictures such as buildings and palm trees on the flannel.
4. Cover the front of each flannelgraph figure on lightweight fabric interfacing. Use fine-tip markers to color or outline the figures.
5. Cut pictures from old catalogs or old Sunday school curriculum. Glue small squares of felt or sandpaper to the backs of the pictures to turn them into flannelgraph pieces.
6. Use an entire flat box, such as a pizza box, to make a two-sided display for use on a table-top. Cover both halves of the inside. Open it slightly and place it on a table. Store figures in the box after using them.

SS3826

Cardboard Tube Figures

Materials
Two cardboard tubes (4$\frac{1}{2}$" long)
Puppet patterns (page 24)
Crayons or markers
Scissors
Glue

Adult Preparation
1. Make copies of patterns on page 24.
2. Use a paper cutter rather than scissors to cut out patterns for a large class or group of children.

Instructions
1. Color each figure.
2. If not already cut out, cut along the heavy black outlines.
3. Glue each figure to a cardboard tube. The back edges will overlap slightly. Dab some glue under the overlapping edges and hold there until glue starts to dry.
4. Use these figures as part of a tabletop scene to tell a Bible story, or wear a figure on the middle fingers of your hand as a puppet.

Other Idea
1. If you have extra time, draw your own pictures to make other Bible figures out of cardboard tubes.

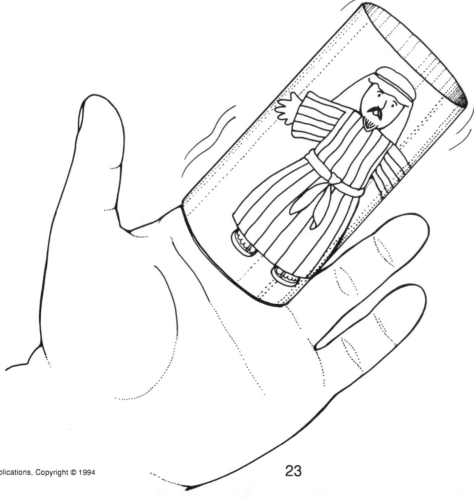

SS3826

Puppet Patterns

SS3826

Bible Story Sandpaper Pictures

Materials

Fine-grain light-brown sandpaper
Fluorescent or brightly colored crayons
Toaster oven

Instructions

1. Draw a Bible-time scene on the rough side of the sandpaper. Pictures of desert scenes work especially well because the sandpaper looks like a sandy background.
2. Place the sandpaper with the drawing faceup on the rack of a toaster oven on low heat (approximately 200 degrees) for a few seconds. Remove sandpaper when the crayon design begins to melt slightly. (An adult needs to supervise this activity carefully so you don't get burned!)

Other Ideas

1. Frame the picture by gluing it on a piece of black construction paper.
2. Tape a piece of yarn to the back to hang the picture on the wall.

Joseph's Coat of Many Colors

Materials
Bible-time coat pattern (page 27)
Colored chalk, crayons, or markers
Chalk fixative such as buttermilk or hair spray (Buy hair spray in an environmentally safe non-aerosol bottle.)
Paintbrush
Scissors

Adult Preparation
1. Copy the coat pattern on page 27. (You may wish to enlarge or reduce pattern.)

Instructions
1. Color the coat.
2. Cut out the coat.
3. If using chalk, paint a bit of buttermilk on the coat or ask an adult to help you spray the project with hair spray in a well-ventilated area. (This will keep the chalk from rubbing off.)
4. Let the coat dry. Use it to tell the Bible story of Joseph and his multicolored coat (Genesis 37).

Other Ideas
1. Trace around the cutout coat on black construction paper. Decorate it, using fluorescent crayons or chalk to make a unique coat.
2. Decorate the coat with other ornamental trims, such as glitter glue or rickrack.

SS3826

Bible-Time Coat Pattern

SS3826

Sidewalk Chalk "Graffiti"

Materials
Regular or large colored chalk intended for drawing on sidewalks

Adult Preparation
1. Find a place such as a sidewalk or cement driveway where a child (or class of children) can draw.
2. Though chalk will rub off later, get permission in advance to draw on this area.

Instructions
1. Use chalk to draw simple pictures and write cheerful messages on the pavement.
2. Write Bible verses or draw pictures that will make people happy by reminding them of God's love.

Other Ideas
1. Chalk may be washed off later with water or will eventually rub off over time, especially if it rains.
2. If you are sure they won't mind your writing on their property, surprise someone with special sidewalk messages, such as for "Grandparents' Day."
3. Decorate a chalkboard or a small miniature slate with messages, or use a chalkboard to tell a "chalk-talk" Bible story to younger children.
4. Decorate a piece of mural paper with messages and pictures. Hang it on a bulletin board or in a hallway for everyone to see.

SS3826

Fabric-Crayons Wall Hanging

Materials

Fabric crayons (available at fabric or craft stores)
Several sheets of white typing paper
White or light-colored fabric (synthetic blend cotton)
Fabric markers or permanent markers
Scissors
Iron and ironing board
Sheets of newspaper
Glue
Wooden dowel or stick
Yarn

Adult Preparation

1. Cut a piece of light-colored fabric into a rectangle. (Base the size of the rectangle on whether the child wants to make a miniature wall hanging or one the size of typing paper.)
2. Cut or break the stick or dowel to a size to fit the fabric. (If necessary, use a saw and some sandpaper to cut and smooth the dowel.)

Instructions

1. Use fabric crayons to draw a picture on a sheet of white paper.
2. The picture can be of something you like about God's creation or something that reminds you of a Bible story.
3. Brush or blow off excess crayon flecks.

Adult Follow-Up

1. Place fabric on a stack of newspaper sheets covered with a sheet of white paper.
2. Lay the paper with the drawing on it facedown on the fabric.
3. Set the iron on the cotton setting.
4. Put another clean sheet of paper between the iron and the paper with the drawing on it.
5. Iron with a steady pressure over the entire drawing until the image becomes slightly visible through the back of the paper. Don't move the iron too much or the design may blur, but don't let the iron scorch the fabric.
6. Carefully remove the picture. The image will be transferred to the fabric. The pattern may be used again later to make other projects.
7. Help each child write words on the fabric, using fabric markers or permanent markers.
8. Help each child overlap the top edge of the fabric around a stick or dowel. Glue the overlapped edge in place.
9. Cut a piece of yarn and tie it to both ends of the stick or dowel to hang the wall hanging.

Other Ideas

1. If you have time, cut a decorative fringe along the bottom.
2. To make a miniature wall hanging, attach the project to a wooden craft stick.

SS3826

Bible Verse Puzzle Card

Materials

Lightweight cardboard (or a blank jigsaw puzzle board from a craft or stationery store)
Markers or crayons
Scissors
Envelope
Bible

Instructions

1. If the puzzle is not precut, cut a piece of cardboard into the shape you want, such as a rectangle, square, or heart.
2. Write a favorite Bible verse on the cardboard or puzzle. You may want to draw little pictures in place of some words.
3. If the puzzle is not precut, cut the cardboard into at least five puzzle pieces. Don't cut them too small, or they might rip.
4. Carefully pull apart any puzzle pieces which are attached together.
5. Put the pieces in an envelope and give or send the puzzle to a friend with a note. Tell the person to put the puzzle together to discover a message from the Bible.

Other Idea

1. Use rubber stamps and ink pads or decorative stickers to represent words from a Bible verse.

SS3826

Styrofoam™ Meat Tray Printing

Materials
Styrofoam™ meat tray
Scissors
Ballpoint pen or sharpened pencil
Poster paint (blue if doing ocean scene)
Paintbrush
Paper plate or sheet of white or light-colored paper
Yarn
Clear tape
Marker

Step 1

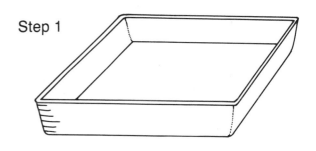

Instructions
1. Cut off and remove the curved sides of the meat tray so that it lies flat.
2. Using a ballpoint pen or sharp pencil, engrave a simple design on the tray. Draw something, such as fish, that reminds you of God's creation.
3. Paint the meat tray.
4. To make a print of your design, carefully place the tray, painted side down, on a paper plate or sheet of paper. Press and rub gently over the back of the meat tray to transfer the painted design. Remove the meat tray.
5. Use a marker or ballpoint pen to write a message, such as "God made the fish of the sea," on the picture after the paint dries.
6. To hang the picture on a wall, tape yarn to the back of it.

Step 2

Step 3

Steps 4-6

blue

God made the fish of the sea!

Paper Plate Baby Beds

Materials
Small paper plate (you will need two if making a lid for baby Moses' basket)
Crayons or markers
Scissors
Stapler and staples
Clear tape
Brad fastener
Yellow yarn (for Baby Jesus)

Instructions
1. Cut a paper plate in half.
2. Place the plate halves together on top of each other to form a pocket shape for the "bed."
3. Staple the plate halves along the bottom rounded edges.
4. Copy, color, and cut out the baby pattern above to represent a baby from the Bible, such as Baby Jesus or Moses.
5. Draw details on the outside of the plate halves.
6. If you're making Baby Jesus in the manger, place yarn in the bed for hay. Tape the baby on the hay, making sure He can be seen.
7. If you're making baby Moses in his basket, make a lid from another paper plate. Follow the same directions for cutting and stapling, to make the lid. Use a brad fastener to attach the lid to the basket as shown in the illustration. The lid will open and close.
8. Use the baby bed to retell the Bible story you have chosen.

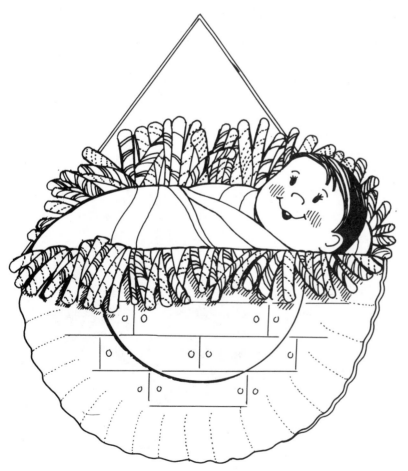

Paper Plate Noah's Ark

Materials
Paper plate
Scissors
Stapler and staples
Construction paper
Crayons or markers

Instructions
1. Cut a paper plate in half.
2. Place the plate halves together on top of each other to form a pocket shape for the ark.
3. Staple the plate halves along the bottom rounded edges.
4. Draw simple shapes of several different animals on construction paper. (Make sure the animals will fit in the ark.) Cut out two of each.
5. Color and draw details on the animals. Then place them in the ark.

Other Ideas
1. An easy method for making animals is to trace or copy them from coloring books or storybooks.
2. Use the animal stencil patterns on pages 38-39.
3. Enlarge the animals on a copier.
4. Glue tiny plastic wiggle eyes on the animals' heads.

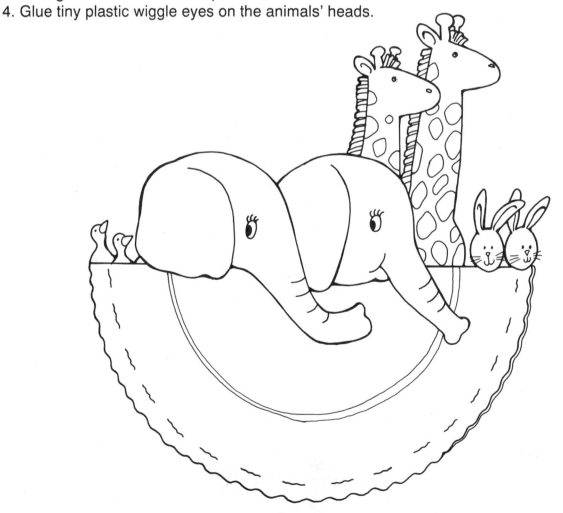

SS3826

Sponge Painting

Materials
Flat sponges (or precut sponge shapes from craft stores)
Scissors
Poster paint
Flat, small pan (such as a frozen food container or aluminum pie pan)
White or light-colored sheets of construction paper
Markers

Adult Preparation
1. If sponges are not precut, cut out one or more simple shapes of things for which we thank God or which remind us of God's creation, such as animals, trees, or flowers.
2. Pour a small amount of poster paint into flat container or pan.

Instructions
1. Dip one flat side of a sponge shape into the paint in the pan.
2. Press sponge shape on paper to stamp a figure. Put several figures on the page.
3. After the paint dries, write these or similar words on the paper: "Thank You, Lord!"
4. Draw background scenery around the figures.

Other Ideas
1. If there is enough time, let each child cut out some sponge shapes.
2. Use the patterns on pages 37-40 to make the sponge shapes. If necessary, enlarge the patterns.
3. Cut shapes from Styrofoam™ meat trays. Use these shapes to make prints on the picture.
4. Use the sponge shapes to decorate greeting cards made from folded construction paper.
5. Use sponges and watered-down fabric paint to decorate T-shirts and hats.

Thank You, Lord!

SS3826

Stenciling Techniques

Materials
Stencil patterns (pages 37-40)
Carbon paper
Pencil
Heavy paper, tagboard, or sheet of clear plastic (available at hobby or industrial plastic shops)
Sharp hobby or utility knife
$\frac{1}{4}$" thick plate of glass or stack of newspapers
Black permanent marker or special stencil pencil (available at hobby or graphics shops)

Adult Preparation
1. Copy patterns on pages 37-40. You may want to enlarge or reduce them.
2. Place each pattern page on carbon paper which is facedown over heavy paper or tagboard.
3. Trace the patterns so they will transfer to the heavy paper or tagboard.
4. Place heavy paper or tagboard over a plate of glass or stack of newspapers to protect the surface underneath.
5. Use a hobby knife to cut out the center area of each stencil.
6. You now have a sturdy stencil which children can use to make the fun projects described on pages 36-42.

Other Ideas
1. Sheets of clear, sturdy plastic, such as Mylar™, make durable stencils. Rather than making paper copies first, you may place the clear plastic directly over the patterns to trace them. Use a black permanent marker or a stencil pen (which can be rubbed off later) to trace the pattern. Cut the marked stencil over glass or newspapers to protect the surface underneath. If necessary, place a sheet of white paper under the glass on the table so you can see the outlined pattern more clearly as you cut it out.
2. Try to cut the pattern directly on the marked lines, cutting toward yourself.
3. Try to cut with smooth, unbroken lines, but don't worry if you make a mistake and cut through in the wrong place. Just use transparent tape on both sides of the mistake to fix it, then recut it.
4. The stencils may be used with a variety of materials, such as paper to make gift cards, pictures, posters, story booklets, and to decorate novelty items and gifts such as T-shirts. Fill in the center of the stencil with paint by dabbing it on with a sponge or with crayons or markers.

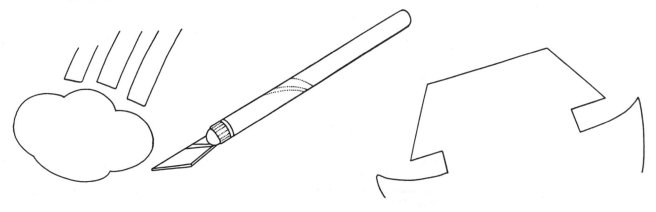

Creation Mural Class Project

Materials
Precut stencils (See pages 35, 37-40. You may prefer to buy stencils at a craft store.)
Mural paper
Scissors
Crayons or markers
Masking tape or thumbtacks
Pencils

Adult Preparation
1. Cut stencils from pages 37-40. Follow directions on page 35 to make and cut stencils, or buy premade stencils.
2. Cut mural paper and tape it to a wall or on a table, or tack it to a bulletin board within the children's reach.
3. Hand out stencil pages to children.

Instructions
1. Place stencil page on mural paper.
2. Trace inside the stencil figure you want. You may want to ask someone to help you hold the stencil in place while you trace inside the figure.
3. Remove the stencil and color the shape.
4. Take turns with friends adding stencil figures to the paper to make a big nature scene like a park.
5. Write a message on the poster, such as "God made our beautiful world!"

Other Ideas
1. If you have enough time, do this project at one session, allowing each child several minutes to use the stencils.
2. If time is limited, let each child in the group color, using only one stencil at each session. This method works well when a child has a few minutes such as when arriving, just before leaving, or after finishing another project.

God made me a beautiful world!

Stencil Patterns

SS3826

Stencil Patterns

SS3826

Stencil Patterns

SS3826

Noah's Ark Stencil Patterns

Stand-Up Critters

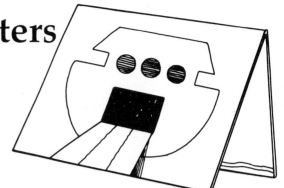

Materials
Construction paper
Scissors
Ink stamp pads
Fine-line markers or crayons

Instructions
1. Cut and fold small pieces of paper to make stand-up cards.
2. Press a finger on an ink pad and make a fingerprint on the front of each card. Let the ink dry.
3. Use markers or crayons to add details to make the fingerprint into an animal. Make a pair of each type of animal.
4. Cut and fold a larger piece of paper to make Noah's ark. Draw a boat on the outside of the card. Cut and fold open a flap for the door and draw a ramp.

Other Ideas
1. Each card will take several minutes to make, so this project may need to be completed during several short sessions.
2. This project works well with a group, each child making a pair of animals. An adult may want to make the ark ahead of time. Set the completed project on a counter or table to display it.
3. Plain white index cards may be substituted for construction paper.
4. Other ideas include: rubber-ink animal stamps, animal stickers, tiny animal erasers, or animal-shaped crackers (cookies). Use glue to attach the erasers or crackers to the cards.
5. You might want to use the animal and ark stencils on pages 38-40 for this project.
6. Write messages such as "All creatures great and small, the Lord God made them all!" on the cards. Then use them to tell the creation story.
7. The cards make fun gift tags or greeting cards.
8. Add decorative trims such as tiny plastic wiggle eyes, dot stickers, or hole punch paper dots to make antennae, eyes, etc., for animals.

Stenciled Sweatshirt

Materials
Sweatshirt (or T-shirt)
Noah's ark stencil (page 40)
Fabric pastels (from fabric or craft store)
Shirt cardboard backing or sheet of cardboard to fit inside shirt
Iron and ironing board
Fabric pen

Adult Preparation
1. Wash and dry shirt to preshrink it.
2. Precut stencil according to directions on page 35.
3. Slide sheet of cardboard inside shirt.

Instructions
1. Use stencils and a fabric pen to outline Noah's ark design on the front of your shirt.
2. Color the design, using special fabric pastels, or draw your own design. (Keep your design simple.)

Adult Follow-Up
1. Remove cardboard backing from the shirt.
2. Place a piece of plain white paper over the pastel design and iron over it to make the colors absorb into the fabric. (For more specific information, see the instructions provided with your fabric pastels box.)
3. Use a permanent fabric pen to write an inspirational message on the shirt, such as "God keeps His promises!" (Older children may do this with your help.)

Other Idea
1. Decorate a tote bag, backpack, hat, or fabric sun visor to match the design on your shirt. Then enjoy wearing your matching outfit!

SS3826

"Noah's Ark Animals" Shoe Decorations

Materials
Shoe decoration patterns (page 44)
Heavy paper
Scissors
Crayons or markers
Hole punch

Adult Preparation
1. Copy patterns on page 44 on heavy paper. Make two copies of each animal head for each child.
2. Cut out the animal heads if each child is not getting the whole page.

Instructions
1. Color each pair of matching animal heads.
2. Cut out each pair of animals.
3. Fold back on the broken lines on each animal.
4. Punch holes where indicated on each animal.
5. Ask an adult to help you attach the animals to the laces on a pair of your shoes.
6. Wearing these shoe decorations will remind you of the animals coming two by two into Noah's ark.

Other Ideas
1. If you use lightweight paper, glue the patterns on thin cardboard.
2. Make the patterns from colored tagboard, colored paper, or thin, colored art foam rubber.
3. Make your own animal designs or use patterns from coloring books.
4. Cover the animals with clear adhesive plastic to protect them and make them more durable.
5. Decorate the animals with plastic wiggle eyes, yarn for manes, felt scraps or pom-poms for ears and noses, etc.
6. Make extra pairs of shoe decorations for your friends.

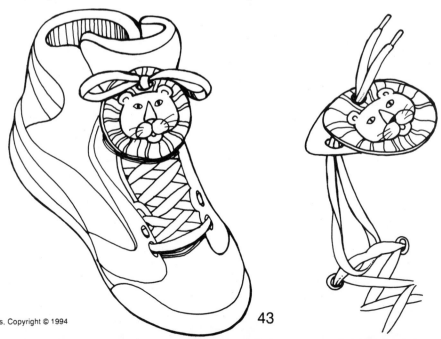

SS3826

Shoe Decoration Patterns

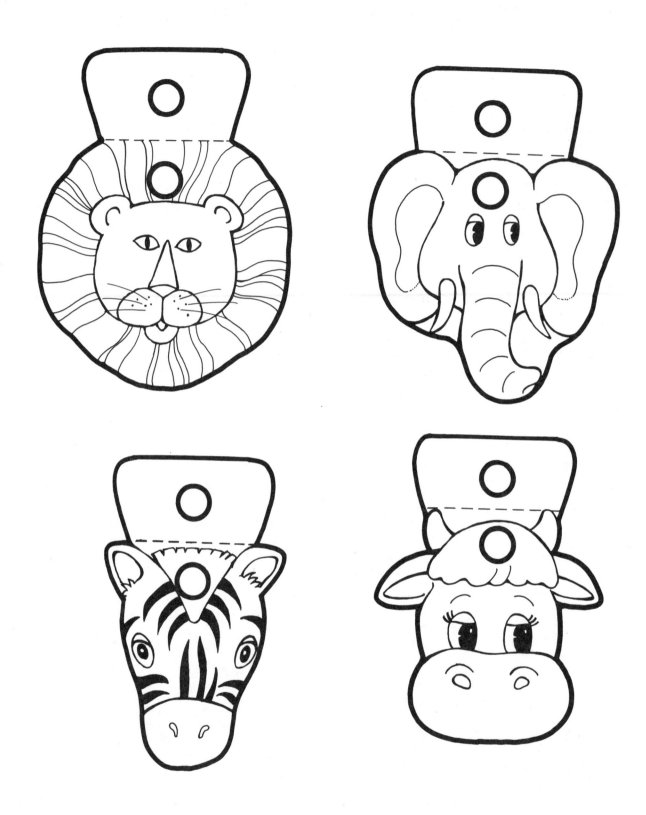

(Make two copies of each animal for each pair of shoes.)

"Animal-Pair" Shoes

Materials
Inexpensive pair of plain-colored canvas tennis shoes
Fabric paint or fabric markers (or permanent markers)
Shoe decorations made from suggestions on pages 43-44
Pencils

Instructions
1. Plan how you want to decorate shoes to remind you of Noah's ark (Genesis 6–8).
2. Draw simple sketches of small animals and an ark on the shoes and print on them "Two by Two." Let ink or paint dry thoroughly before wearing the shoes.
3. You may want to decorate your shoes to match animal designs; for example, use a black marker on white tennis shoes to draw zebra stripes. If you made matching animal shoe decorations, attach them to the laces.

Other Ideas
1. If you only have a few minutes for this project, keep the design very simple.
2. Add decorative trims by using craft glue to attach braided yarn for tails, manes, etc., pom-poms and felt scraps to make little animals, etc. Or use glitter fabric paint to make fancy outlines on the shoes.
3. You may want to decorate another pair of shoes for a friend or a younger brother or sister.

SS3826

"Noah's Ark Animal" Visors

Materials

Inexpensive plastic sun visor (available at craft stores). Get a small size for a young child.
Animal visor patterns (page 47)
Scraps of heavy paper, cardboard, or colored tagboard
Scissors
Decorative trims (craft feathers, felt scraps, large plastic wiggle eyes, fake eyelashes, etc.)
Craft glue or low-temperature glue gun and glue sticks

Adult Preparation

1. Make copies on heavy paper of the cat and duck parts patterns from page 47.
2. You may wish to have two children make matching pairs of animals to act out the Noah's ark story.

Instructions

1. Cut out the parts for a duck or cat. If the pieces are flimsy, glue them on cardboard or tagboard to make them sturdier. Make other noses, ears, etc., if you want to make a different kind of animal.
2. Use craft glue to attach the parts to the visor. Add other decorative trims. With an adult's help, you may use a low-temperature glue gun. (A high-temperature glue gun may melt the plastic!) Hold pieces in place briefly until they begin to dry.
3. Wear your animal visor to remind you that God created all animals. You and a friend may make matching animal visors to wear to remind you of Noah's ark.

Other Ideas

1. Cut a visor from colored art foam rubber, which may be purchased at craft stores. Punch holes at the back of the visor, attach yarn through the holes, then tie the visor to fit your head.
2. Beaks, ears, etc., may also be cut from art foam rubber even if you use a plastic visor for the base.
3. If using paper, cardboard, or tagboard for the features, protect and make the pieces sturdier by covering them with clear adhesive plastic.
4. Use a fabric painter's cap or baseball cap instead of a visor.
5. These visors make great gifts for younger brothers and sisters and are fun to use in a play or skit about Noah's ark.

SS3826

Animal Visor Patterns

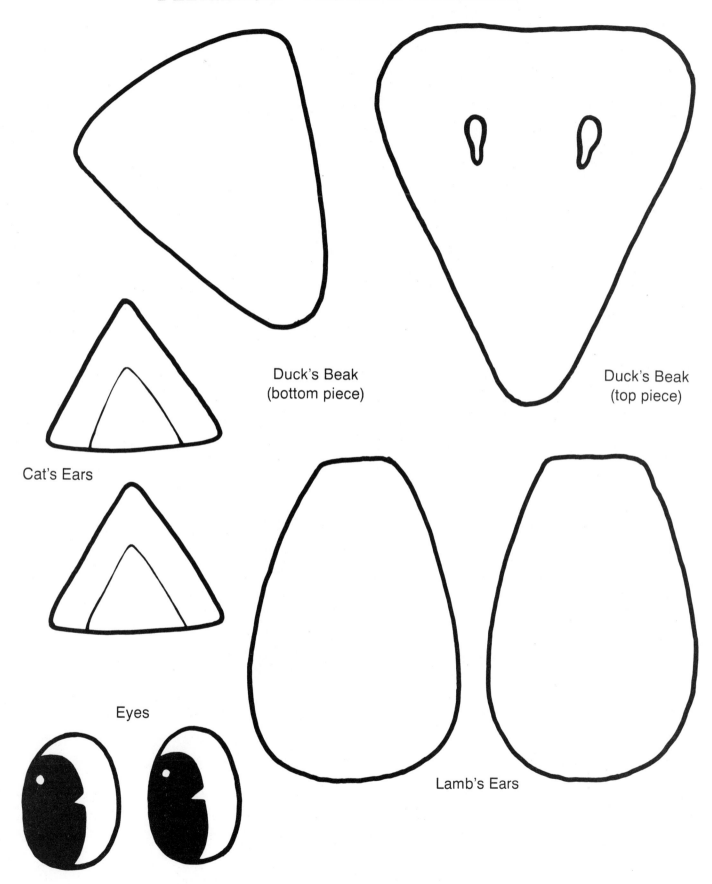

Duck's Beak
(bottom piece)

Duck's Beak
(top piece)

Cat's Ears

Eyes

Lamb's Ears

SS3826

Lamb Cap

Materials
White baseball cap
Lamb eyes and ears patterns (page 47)
Permanent black marker
Black and white felt scraps or large plastic wiggle eyes
White felt scraps
Scissors
Decorative trims (fake eyelashes and cotton ball or pom-pom for nose)
Extra bits of cotton or cotton balls
Craft glue or low-temperature glue gun and glue sticks

Adult Preparation
1. Copy the lamb eyes and ears patterns on page 47.
2. Plan for one pair of items for each child's hat.

Instructions
1. Cut out the patterns and use a black marker to trace around them on felt to make eyes and ears. (Or use large plastic eyes.)
2. Glue features and decorative trims to the baseball cap as shown. Glue bits of cotton to the hat and to the outside of the ears for lamb's wool.
3. Wear the hat to act out Bible stories involving lambs, such as the Christmas story. The hat is also a good reminder that the Lord is the Good Shepherd who cares for you. If a friend makes a matching hat, wear them together as a reminder that the animals came in pairs onto Noah's ark.

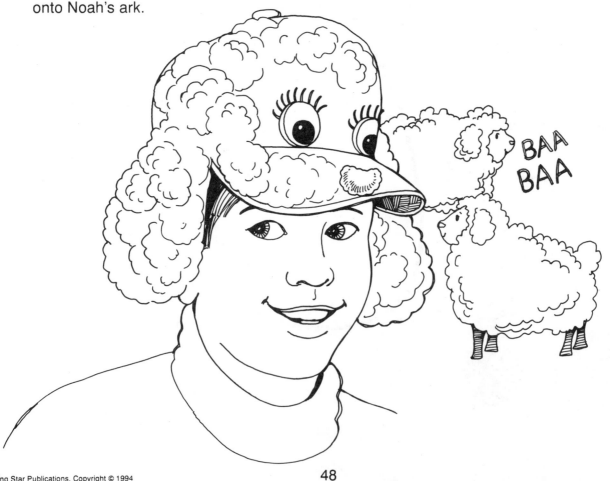

"Son"shine Visor

Materials

Inexpensive plastic or fabric sun visor (available at most craft stores)
Decorative paint or fabric paint (in squeeze bottles) or fast-drying paint pens that work on plastic
  surfaces

Instructions

1. Use paint to decorate the visor with a summer sunshine scene. (Keep the design simple
   and easy so your paint will dry quickly and won't smear so easily.)
2. Write these words on the visor: "I'm a "Son"shine kid!"
3. When you wear the visor, it will show everyone that Jesus, the Son of God, brings sunshine into your life!

SS3826

Fabric Pastels Design T-Shirt

Materials

Child-sized white or light colored T-shirt
Fabric pastels (available at fabric or craft stores)
Sun pattern (page 51)
Iron and ironing board
Sheet of sturdy cardboard or T-shirt backing (available at fabric or craft store)
Several sheets of white typing paper
Black crayon

Adult Preparation

1. Wash and dry the T-shirt to preshrink it.
2. Copy the sun pattern and trace over it with a black crayon.
3. Pull the T-shirt over a sheet of cardboard or cardboard frame so the shirt will lie flat.
4. Place the sun pattern facedown over the front of the shirt.
5. Iron over the pattern so the design transfers to the front of the shirt. (Some of the black crayon will transfer directly to the shirt to make a light-gray outline. Set the iron on low heat to do the transfer so the paper won't burn.) The words which are backwards on the pattern will be readable when transferred.

Instructions

1. Use fabric pastels to color the sun design and to trace over the words on the T-shirt.
2. Place a blank sheet of white typing paper directly over the colored design. With an adult's help, iron over the paper on high (cotton) heat to warm the pastel design so it sets into the fabric. (See the directions on the fabric pastels box for more information.) Remove the cardboard backing.
3. Wear your T-shirt to remind you that Jesus, the SON of God, brings sunshine into your life. (If you already made the visor on page 49, you may want to wear it when you wear this shirt.)

I'm a "SON"shine Kid!

51

Fabric Pastels Backpack/Tote Bag

Materials

Fabric backpack/tote bag (available at fabric or craft stores)
Fabric pastels (available at fabric or craft stores)
Sun pattern (page 51)
Iron and ironing board
Sheet of sturdy cardboard
Sheet of white typing paper

Adult Preparation

1. Wash and dry the backpack or tote bag to preshrink it. Pastels will absorb more easily into washed fabric.
2. Copy the sun pattern on page 51.
3. Insert a sheet of cardboard into the bag so it will lie flat.
4. Place the sun pattern over the front of the bag.
5. Iron over the pattern so the design transfers to the front of the bag. (Some of the black ink will transfer directly onto the bag to make a light-gray outline which will wash out later. Set the iron on low heat so the paper won't burn.) The words which are backwards on the pattern will be readable when transferred.

Instructions

1. Use fabric pastels to color the sun design and to trace over the words on the tote bag.
2. Place a blank sheet of white typing paper directly over the colored design. With an adult's help, iron over the paper on high heat to warm the design so it sets into the fabric. (See directions on the fabric pastels box for more information.) Remove the cardboard.
3. Use your backpack or tote bag for books, shopping, etc. If you made the visor on page 49 or the T-shirt on page 50, use this bag when you wear those other items to the beach, to the shopping mall, or wherever you go!

Celebration Hair Bow

Materials

Premade fabric hair bow, clear plastic vinyl film (and iron), or cellophane gift wrap
Scissors
Craft glue or low temperature glue gun and glue sticks
Decorative trims (colorful curling ribbon or fabric ribbon, glitter glue pens, beads, sequins, small pom-poms, etc.)
Hair clip (if you're not using a premade bow)

Instructions

1. Begin with a premade fabric hair bow, or use plastic vinyl film or cellophane to make a see-through double-sided bow that you can stuff with decorative items such as beads, sequins, or stars. (An adult will need to help you iron the edges of the bow to seal it.)
2. Stuff a vinyl bow with decorative items or glue the items to the outside of a fabric or cellophane bow. Gather and tie the center of the bow with curled ribbon as shown. Glue or tie a hair clip to the back of the bow if the bow isn't premade.
3. Use a glitter glue pen to write "Celebrate God's Love!" on the outside. Let the bow dry thoroughly.
4. Wear the bow to Sunday school, church, parties, or other places to remind everyone of the joy of experiencing God's love. You may want to give this bow as a gift.

Running Shoes Projects

Materials
Shoes pattern (page 55)
Crayons or markers
Scissors
Glue
12" x 18" sheet of construction paper

Adult Preparation
1. Copy the running shoes pattern on page 55.
2. Each child should get one complete pair.

Instructions
1. Color and cut out the running shoes.
2. To make a greeting card, fold construction paper in half as shown.
3. Glue the shoe with the first part of the verse on the outside of the card.
4. Glue the other shoe to the inside of the card.
5. Add your own words, such as "Get well soon!" or other words to cheer someone. Then give or send the card to someone who is sick or sad.

Other Ideas
1. Use this idea to make a card for someone who is a runner or jogger, such as a parent, for Mother's Day or Father's Day.
2. If you have extra time, decorate the shoes with glitter glue pens.
3. Fold along the glued heel of the shoe and leave the back "wing" unglued to create a three-dimensional effect on the card.
4. Tape a piece of yarn to the backs of the shoes to make a mobile to hang from the ceiling.
5. If you have extra time, punch holes in the shoes and lace yarn through them for shoelaces. Yarn will go through the holes more easily if you attach clear tape on the ends to keep it from unraveling. Laced shoes may be attached together as shown. Dangle them from a nail or peg as a wall decoration, or tack them to a bulletin board.

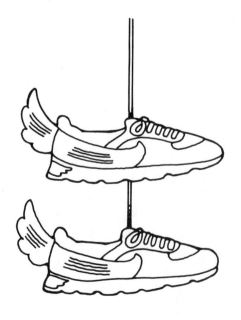

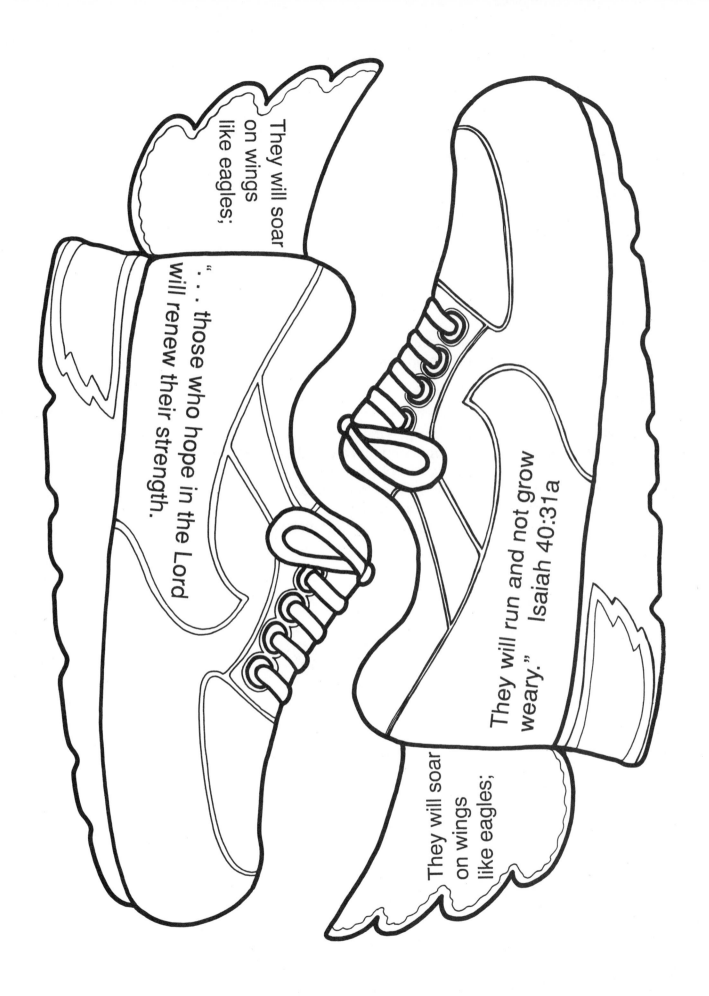

They will soar
on wings
like eagles;

" . . . those who hope in the Lord
will renew their strength.

They will run and not grow
weary."   Isaiah 40:31a

They will soar
on wings
like eagles;

55

SS3826

"Jesus Loves Me" Mirror

Materials
Small round mirror (available at craft stores)
Hand mirror pattern (page 57)
Construction paper
Glue
Lightweight cardboard
Scissors
Markers or crayons
Yarn (black, brown, yellow, red)

Adult Preparation
1. Copy the hand mirror pattern on page 57.
2. If you have time, glue the pattern on cardboard.

Instructions
1. Color and cut out the hand mirror.
2. If not already done so by an adult, glue the pattern to cardboard and cut it out.
3. Glue construction paper to the front and trim along the edges.
4. Glue a small mirror to the front to reflect your face.
5. Glue yarn around the edges of the mirror to represent your hair.
6. Draw your clothing on the front of the handle.
7. When you use this mirror, remember that Jesus loves you just as you are.

Other Ideas
1. Before gluing on the small mirror, cover the project with clear adhesive plastic to protect it.
2. If you don't have a real mirror to use, substitute a round circle of aluminum foil.

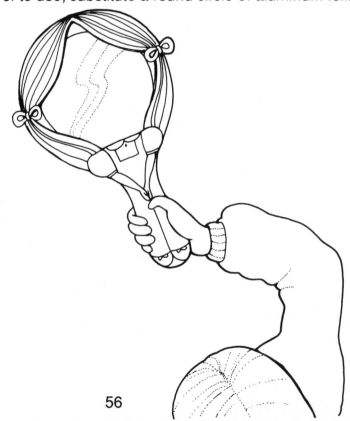

Hand Mirror Pattern
(back side)

SS3826

Class Autographs T-Shirt

Materials

White or light-colored T-shirt
Permanent ink fabric marking pens (in a variety of colors)
Sheet of cardboard or T-shirt backing

Adult Preparation

1. Buy a T-shirt to fit the person to whom it will be given.
2. Wash and dry the shirt to preshrink and prepare it.
3. Slip cardboard or backing inside the shirt so it will lie flat.

Instructions

1. Use marking pens to sign your name, write encouraging messages, and draw pictures on the shirt.
2. Work together with friends to decorate the shirt.
3. Give this shirt to someone, such as a classmate who is ill.

Other Ideas

1. Decorate a shirt to present to a volunteer assistant or teacher as a thank-you gift.
2. Each child may bring a shirt which all the other children autograph as a souvenir of a memorable experience. This is a fun activity for the last day of summer camp, vacation Bible school, the end of the school year, etc.
3. Rather than making shirts, students may decorate mural paper to make class posters, compile autograph books, or sign novelty items such as scarves, bandanas, baseball hats, or stuffed toys.

Balloon Bouquet

Materials
Several large balloons (in a variety of colors)
Plastic balloon sticks (available at craft or party supply stores)
Permanent markers or quick-drying, oil-based paint pens (that will write on rubber or plastic)
Yarn or ribbon
Scissors

Instructions
1. Blow up several balloons. If necessary, ask a friend or an adult to help you blow them up and tie knots in the ends.
2. Write encouraging messages and draw simple pictures on the balloons.
3. Have someone help you tie the balloons to plastic sticks.
4. Tie a piece of ribbon or yarn around several sticks to make a "bouquet" to give to someone.

Other Ideas
1. Decorate the balloons and give them to a classmate who is ill or to an ill church member.
2. Decorate balloons as a gift or centerpiece for a special day, such as Mother's Day or Father's Day.
3. A group or class may work together on this project, each child decorating one balloon and the teacher or parent putting together the bouquet.
4. Go on a field trip with your class, family, or group of friends to deliver balloon bouquets to a hospital or nursing home to give balloons to patients.

SS3826

Balloon Gift Basket

Materials

5" round balloon
5 chenille stems (pipe cleaners)
Ruler
Scissors
Plastic berry basket (from grocery store or fruit stand)
Items to fill the basket (miniature teddy bears and dolls, little flowers, candy, etc.)
Cloud pattern (from this page)
Clear tape

Adult Preparation

1. Copy the cloud pattern on this page.
2. If the child who does this project is young, you may wish to blow up the balloon and tie a knot in the end of it in advance.
3. Measure and cut four chenille stems each to be 9" long.

Instructions

1. Make a circle from a chenille stem. Attach the other four chenille stems to the circle as shown.
2. Bend and attach the four ends of the straight chenille stems to the four corners of the berry basket.
3. If the balloon is not already blown up, blow it up and ask an adult to help you tie a knot in the end of it.
4. Place the balloon in the chenille stem circle as shown. Tape it securely to the chenille stem.
5. Cut out the cloud and tape it to the side of the balloon.
6. Fill the basket with treats, and give it to someone to cheer him up.

Other Ideas

1. Rather than taping the cloud on, write directly on the balloon with permanent markers or quick-drying, oil-based paint pens. You may want to write on the balloon the name of the person to whom you will give this gift.
2. Wrap treats, such as candies or small cookies, in colored plastic wrap and tie the package with a pretty ribbon before putting it into the basket.
3. If you have extra time, weave yarn or narrow ribbon through the basket to decorate it. Attach extra ribbons to hang down from the basket like streamers.

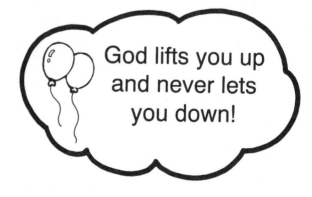

God lifts you up and never lets you down!

Memo Note Clip

Materials

Plastic clip (large paper clip, miniature clothespin, or note clip)
Clear tape
Construction paper
Decorative stickers (with inspirational messages or pictures)
Scissors
Fine-line markers

Instructions

1. Attach a decorative sticker to a plastic clip.
2. If necessary, attach construction paper to the back of the sticker, or mount the sticker on the paper before attaching it to the plastic clip.
3. Give the clip to someone to use as a note clip or a bookmark.

Other Ideas

1. Because these clips are small, they work well as gifts to send through the mail or to enclose with greeting cards.
2. Staple together several small sheets of paper to make a little notepad to go with the clip.
3. To hang up a larger spring-type clip on the refrigerator, attach a strip of magnetic tape to the back.
4. To protect the sticker decoration, cover it with clear adhesive plastic.

Plastic Jewelry and Magnets

Materials
Small sheets of colored molding plastic (available at craft stores)
Jewelry "findings" (tie tack backings, cuff links, earring backs, necklace links, broach pins, hair clips, etc.) or small magnets or strips of magnetic tape
Scissors
Aluminum foil
Cooking oil
Toaster oven
Pot holder
Strong glue (such as E-6000™)

Instructions
1. Cut colored plastic into a small, simple shape such as a square, heart, or cross.
2. You may want to decorate a larger piece with a smaller piece of a different colored plastic.
3. Place the plastic shape on a sheet of aluminum foil greased with cooking oil. Layer the small piece of plastic over the larger piece to decorate the project with a second color.

Adult Follow-Up
1. Preheat the oven to 225 degrees.
2. Place the child's project in the oven. (If the oven has a window, the child will enjoy watching it.)
3. Bake the child's project in an oven for one to two minutes. The longer the plastic is left in the oven, the more it will melt together to look "inlaid." Don't leave it in too long, though, or the plastic will begin to bubble.
4. Use a pot holder to remove the project from the oven. The plastic will be warm, but not too hot to handle. Softened plastic may be molded or textured for further decoration.
5. Place the child's project in cold water to set for three to five seconds. (See directions included with plastic for more information and ideas.)
6. Help the child glue the jewelry findings to the plastic. Or help the child attach a small magnet or strip of magnetic tape to the back of the plastic to make a refrigerator magnet.

Other Ideas
1. Write words or draw on the plastic with oil-based paint pens or other permanent markers.
2. Decorate the projects with beads, sequins, glitter, etc.

My sister wearing jewelry I made for her!

Gift Mug

Materials
Inexpensive plain-colored plastic mug (available at craft stores or in the housewares department at discount stores)
Fast-drying, oil-based paint pens

Instructions
1. Use paint pens to decorate the outside of the mug. (Don't decorate too close to the rim.)
2. Decorate the mug with messages, such as "My cup overflows with God's love!" or write an inspirational Bible verse. You may want to personalize the mug by writing the person's name on it.
3. Give this gift to someone to use as a kitchen mug, vase, or pencil holder.

Other Ideas
1. Use little stencils to help you paint and decorate the mug. Make your own stencils or buy premade plastic stencils at a craft store.
2. Decorate the mug by using glitter paint pens.
3. Fill the mug with small gifts, such as candy, crayons, cute erasers, and colored pencils.
4. Wrap the gift-filled mug with clear-colored plastic or colored cellophane wrap, and tie it with a big gift bow.
5. Make several of these projects with friends or family as gifts to deliver to people who are sick or sad.

Toy with a Message

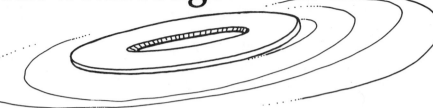

Materials
Miniature skimmer ring or Frisbee™
Quick-drying, oil-based paint pen
Decorative stickers

Instructions
1. Use a paint pen to write on the plastic skimmer ring or Frisbee™, a message such as "God's love is like a never-ending circle for you and me!"
2. Decorate the toy with cute stickers.
3. Give this toy to someone as a gift, or toss it to a friend to share its special message!

Plastic Gift Container/Ornament

Materials

Clear plastic container (available at craft and party supply stores)
Quick-drying, oil-based paint pens or glitter pens
Tiny treats (novelty erasers, stickers, candies, potpourri mix, etc.)
Thread or narrow ribbon
Scissors

Instructions

1. Decorate the outside of the container. Write encouraging messages, such as "Jesus loves you!" You may wish to personalize the gift by writing the person's name on it.
2. After the ink dries, open the container and fill it with treats.
3. Tie a piece of thread or ribbon to make it into an ornament or to hang it from the ceiling.
4. Give this project as a gift to someone for a special day, such as a birthday, Valentine's Day, or Christmas.

HAPPY BIRTHDAY! Love, Brian

The fruit of the Spirit is LOVE, JOY, PEACE

Jesus loves you!

Jesus is the way

HEARTLAND POTPOURRI MIX

BRIGHT MORNING STAR

KING OF KINGS LORD OF LORDS

SS3826

Treasure Box

Materials

Small wooden box with lid (available at craft or hobby shops)
Dimensional or "puff" paint pens (in squeeze bottles)
Glitter pens
Small scrap of paper
Scissors
Marker or ballpoint pen

Instructions

1. Use paint pens and glitter pens to decorate the outside of the box to make a "treasure" or trinket box. "Puff" paint will puff up when it dries to create a unique effect.
2. Write a message such as "Jesus is my most precious treasure!" on the box.
3. Cut a slip of paper to put inside the box. Write on the paper a Bible verse, such as "But store up for yourselves treasures in heaven . . . . For where your treasure is, there your heart will be also." Matthew 6:20-21.

66   SS3826

"God Rules" Ruler

Materials

6" wooden ruler (available at craft or school supply stores)
Permanent markers or glitter pens
Tiny novelty erasers (shaped hearts, teddy bears, crosses, etc.)
Craft glue

Instructions

1. Use markers and glitter pens to decorate the front and back of the ruler. (Be careful not to cover the measurement lines and numbers on the ruler, since you want it to remain useable for measuring.) Write on it messages such as "God rules! The Lord 'rules' my life!" or "God 'measures' my life with love!"
2. Next to the message on the front, you may want to glue on some little erasers as decorations.
3. Use this ruler in school or Sunday school, or give it as a gift to someone.

Pencil Topper

Materials

Molding plastic or self-hardening, colored clay (available at craft or hobby stores)
Oil-based paint pens
Pencil
Decorative trims (chenille stem, narrow ribbon, small pom-poms, tiny plastic wiggle eyes)
Craft glue
Fine-line markers
Scrap of paper
Scissors

Instructions

1. Make a pencil topper from self-hardening clay or molding plastic. Use a shape such as a heart or teddy bear head.
2. Push the molded shape onto the eraser end of the pencil or attach the shape to the end of a chenille stem (pipe cleaner). Coil the other end of the chenille stem around the eraser end of the pencil.
3. Use a paint pen to write directly on the pencil a message such as "Jesus loves me!" You may prefer to use a marker to write "You're BEARY special!" on a slip of paper. Attach the paper to a teddy bear decoration.
4. Glue decorative trims to the pencil.
5. Use this pencil in school or Sunday school, or surprise someone with this gift!

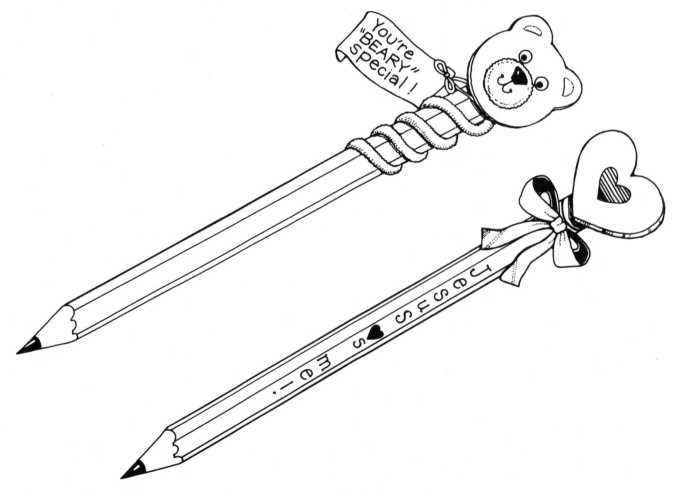

Peelable Plastic Stickers

Materials
Brightly colored glue paint (available at craft or school supply stores)
Plastic wrap or clear sheet of plastic (such as Mylar™)

Instructions
1. Place the sheet of plastic on a table or spread out a piece of plastic wrap to lie flat.
2. Squeeze colored glue paint on the plastic, making shapes such as crosses, flowers, hearts, butterflies, or other Christian symbols. You may want to create decorations with words like "Jesus" and "love."
3. Let the glue paint dry thoroughly. This may take a day or two.
4. Carefully peel the colored stickers off the plastic.
5. Put the stickers on windows, mirrors, refrigerators, plastic school notebooks, lunch boxes, plastic pails, storage bins, etc. You might want to test to make sure the sticker removes easily from the surface before leaving it on too long. Generally, they peel off easily and are reusable.

Other Ideas
1. Buy individual bottles of glue paint or kits which include small bottles in a variety of rainbow colors. Some kits are designed specifically for making stickers and include plastic sheets with outlined patterns and other fun ideas on them.
2. To make sparkly stickers, such as Christmas stars, decorate them with glitter glue after they dry.

SS3826

Plastic Sun Catcher

Materials
Plastic margarine tub lid
Permanent markers
Hole punch
String or clear nylon fishing line
Scissors

Instructions
1. Leave the plastic lid round or cut it into a shape such as a star or rainbow.
2. Punch a hole in the top of the ornament.
3. Use markers to decorate the ornament and write inspirational messages like "Hope!" or "Jesus is my 'SON'shine!" on it.
4. After the project dries, tie string or fishing line through the hole. Hang it in a window to "catch" the rays of the sun. The sun will shine through it and make it look like stained glass.

Other Ideas
1. Use sheets of shrinkable plastic to make the ornaments. Remember that the plastic will shrink to almost half its original size when heated in an oven. These plastic sheets may be purchased in craft stores. Other specific directions for using the plastic are generally provided with the materials. Adult supervision is required when shrinking plastic in the oven, but everyone will enjoy watching the plastic shrink if you have a window on your oven or toaster oven.
2. Experiment with other materials to decorate the sun catcher, such as glitter glue or watered-down colored glue paint.
3. Trace patterns, such as the rainbow on page 72, to make sun catchers.

SS3826

Plastic Key Ring

Materials

Sheets of transparent plastic or shrinkable plastic
Toaster oven
Construction paper
Cookie sheet greased with nonstick spray
Pot holder
Permanent markers
Patterns (page 72)
Scissors
Hole punch
Metal key chain or interlocking key ring

Adult Preparation

1. Copy the patterns on page 72. Cut them apart and give one pattern to each child. If each child has time to make more than one project, hand out copies of all the patterns.
2. Enlarge or reduce the patterns. If you're using shrinkable plastic, the figures will shrink to almost half their original size. (The rainbow and bunny patterns are intentionally designed larger than most key-chain sizes.)

Instructions

1. Place clear plastic over the pattern. Use a dark colored or black permanent marker to trace the design on the plastic.
2. Color the plastic design and cut it out.
3. Punch a hole as shown on the pattern.
4. If you're using shrinkable plastic, an adult will need to help you shrink the plastic on a cookie sheet in an oven.
5. After the project dries (or cools off), attach it to a key chain or key ring.
6. Use the key chain yourself or give it to someone as a gift.

Other Ideas

1. Make key chain decorations from other materials, such as colored tagboard covered with clear adhesive plastic or lightweight balsa wood (available at hobby shops).
2. Decorate the projects with glitter paint, beads, dimensional paint, etc.

Key Ring Patterns

Jesus holds the keys to my heart!

I'm some "bunny" special 'cuz Jesus gives me "lops and lops" of love!

"But as for me and my household, we will serve the LORD." Joshua 24:15c

God keeps His promises!

SS3826

Pressed Flowers Bible Bookmark

Materials

"I'm growing" bookmark pattern (page 74)
Tiny dried flowers, vines, miniature ferns, or leaves
Several sheets of white typing paper
Heavy book
Scissors
Glue
Clear adhesive plastic
Hole punch
Yarn, narrow ribbon, or premade bookmark tassel

Adult Preparation

1. Copy the "I'm growing" bookmark on page 74 and cut out.
2. If the flowers, vines, ferns, or leaves are not already dried, place them between some sheets of paper and press them between the pages of a heavy book. Let plants dry out for several days before having the child do this project.

Instructions

1. Glue pressed flowers and other miniature plants to the bookmark.
2. Cover the bookmark with clear adhesive plastic to protect the dried flowers.
3. Punch a hole where indicated at the top of the bookmark.
4. Insert yarn or ribbon through the hole and tie a bow, or attach a premade bookmark tassel.
5. Use this bookmark to mark your favorite verse in the Bible.

Other Idea

1. Use tiny flower stickers or color the flowers on the bookmark.

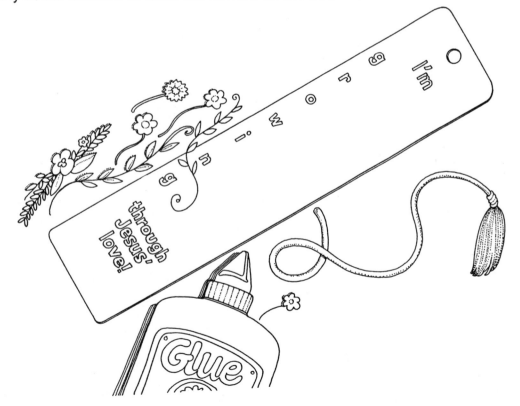

SS3826

Bookmark Patterns

O I'm

g r o w i n g

through Jesus' love!

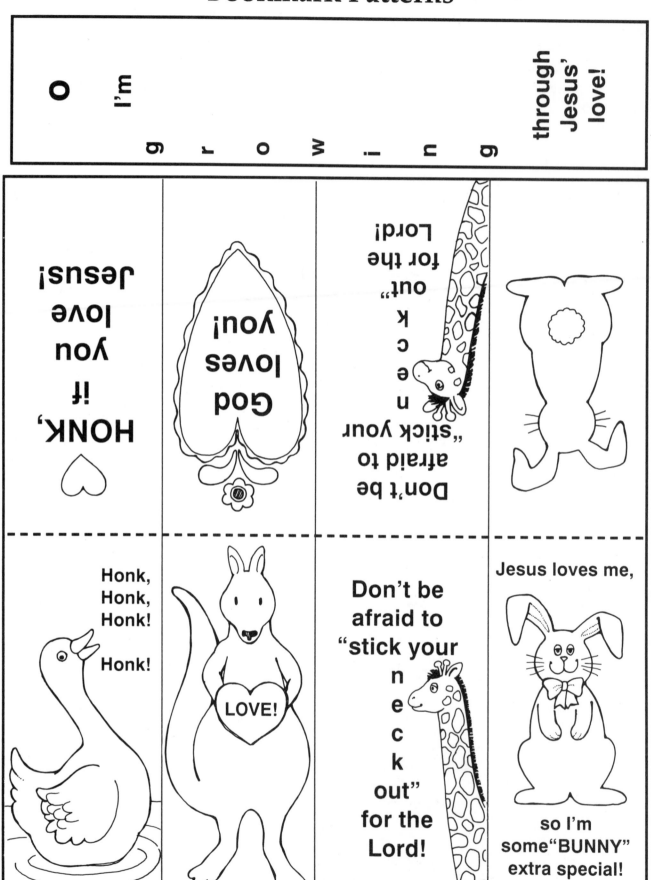

HONK, if you love Jesus!

God loves you!

Don't be afraid to "stick your neck out" for the Lord!

Honk,
Honk,
Honk!

Honk!

LOVE!

Don't be
afraid to
"stick your
n
e
c
k
out"
for the
Lord!

Jesus loves me,

so I'm
some "BUNNY"
extra special!

74

Magnetic Bible Bookmark

Materials
Animal bookmark patterns (page 74)
Crayons or markers
Clear adhesive plastic
Scissors
Strip of magnetic tape
Ruler

Adult Preparation
1. Copy the animal bookmark patterns on page 74. (The bookmark with the flowers and vine on it is for the project on page 73.)
2. Cut apart the bookmarks on the heavy outlines. Plan to have each child decorate one bookmark or, if time allows, each may decorate a set of bookmarks with different animals on them.
3. Measure and cut two strips of magnetic tape, 2" long, for each bookmark.

Instructions
1. Color the bookmark.
2. Have an adult help you cover the front and back of the bookmark with clear adhesive plastic. Trim the edges.
3. Fold the bookmark in half on the broken line with the pictures on the outside. Rub firmly over the folded edge with a fingernail to crease it.
4. Attach a strip of magnetic tape to both the inside bottom edges. There should be a strip on both halves of the inside.
5. Use the bookmark to mark specific verses or passages in your Bible. The sides of the bookmark slip over the page you want to mark. Then, because the two magnetic strips are attracted to each other, the bookmark will stay where you put it.

Other Idea
1. Glue on decorative trims such as yellow feathers on the goose, glitter glue to outline the hearts, tiny plastic wiggle eyes, a cotton ball on the bunny's tail, and a tiny ribbon bow on the bunny's neck.

SS3826

"The Rock" Paperweight

Materials
Smooth rock
Permanent markers or squeeze bottles of dimensional paint

Adult Preparation
1. In advance, find a rock of an appropriate size for a paperweight. If time allows, take the child outside to find a rock.
2. Wash and dry the rock thoroughly so it is clean and ready to decorate.

Instructions
1. Use markers or paint to decorate the rock. Write a message on it, such as "Christ is 'The Solid Rock' of my life!"
2. Let it dry thoroughly, then use it as a paperweight, or give it to someone as a gift.

Other Ideas
1. Spray paint the rock a metallic color, such as gold or silver, before decorating it. Paint in a well-ventilated area with an adult supervising.
2. Decorate the rock with glitter pens to make it sparkle.
3. Use a Bible and a Bible concordance to look up verses which describe Christ as our "rock." Some examples are: Deuteronomy 32:4a–"He is the Rock"; Psalm 89:26b–"The Rock my Savior"; 1 Corinthians 10:4–". . . and that rock was Christ."
4. Discuss why Christ is compared to a rock. (He is solid, firm, strong, and is always there for us, etc.)

76

Miniature Greeting Cards/Gift Tags

Materials

Scraps of construction paper or colored tagboard
Decorative trims (stickers, rubber ink stamps and stamp pads, miniature toy erasers, pretty buttons, etc.)
Glue
Fine-line markers
Scissors
Hole punch
Narrow ribbon or yarn

Instructions

1. Cut little cards as shown. They may be round, rectangular, folded, etc.
2. Decorate the cards with trims, using ideas such as those shown. Use ink stamps to make fingerprint flowers and butterflies on a mini Mother's Day card to attach to a package. Make a gift tag for Father's Day with miniature toy erasers glued onto it.
3. Write messages on the cards.
4. Punch a hole in each card and attach ribbon or yarn to tie it to a gift package.

Other Idea

1. Use these ideas to decorate other gifts, such as bookmarks and recipe cards.

SS3826

Framed Pressed Flowers Picture

Materials
Tiny dried flowers and weeds, greenery such as miniature ferns
Several sheets of white typing paper
Heavy book
Scissors
Small precut colored mat-board frame and backing (available at craft or frame stores)
Wooden toothpick
Glue
Fine-line marker
Clear adhesive plastic
Narrow ribbon
Clear tape

Adult Preparation
1. If the flowers, weeds, and greenery are not already dried, place them between sheets of white paper in the pages of a heavy book.
2. Let flowers, weeds, and greenery press dry for several days.

Instructions
1. Arrange flowers on a sheet of paper and see how they will look behind the frame opening.
2. Glue the flowers and greenery in place, using a toothpick to dab on glue.
3. After the glue dries, ask an adult to help you cover the flowers and the entire area which will be behind the frame with clear adhesive plastic. The plastic will protect the flowers.
4. Glue the frame front and back together to frame the bouquet.
5. On the frame, write a Bible verse or a message such as "Thank You, Lord, for springtime!"
6. Tie a tiny bow and glue it to the bouquet on the outside of the plastic. This will give a three-dimensional appearance to the picture.
7. Tape a piece of ribbon to the back to hang this picture.

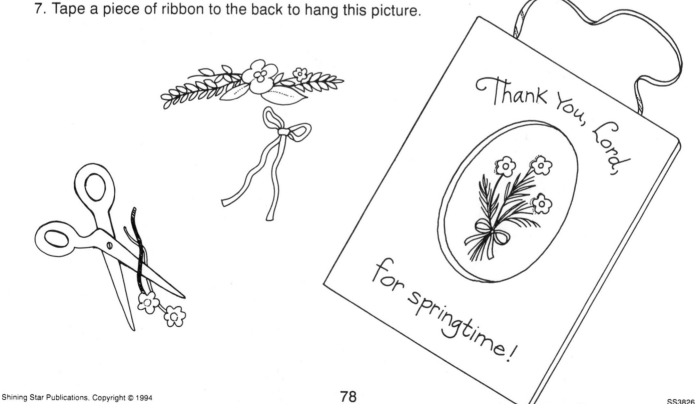

Miniature Scribbler Notepad

Materials

Small piece of rectangular cardboard or colored tagboard (3" x 5" or 4" x 6")
Scissors
Tiny notepad or sheets of paper
Stapler and staples
Yarn or string
Clear tape
Glue
Tiny pencil or sharpened pencil stub
Decorative trims (stickers, rubber design stamps and ink pads, etc.)
Markers

Instructions

1. Cut a cardboard or tagboard rectangle or other shape.
2. Cut paper to the size you want. Staple the pages together.
3. Glue or tape the notepad to the cardboard or tagboard base.
4. Decorate the base with stickers or ink stamps, such as crosses, hearts, and happy faces. Draw simple designs on it too.
5. Tie yarn or string on the eraser end of a pencil and tape the other end of the yarn to the project as shown. The pencil should dangle loosely so it can be used to write on the notepad.
6. Tie yarn or string to the top to hang the notepad on a wall or bulletin board.
7. Use for memos to yourself or your family, or write down Bible verses to memorize each day.

Other Idea

1. Attach strips of magnetic tape to the back of the notepad. Hang it on the refrigerator for a memo pad for your whole family to use.

Cardboard Tube Door Wreath

Materials
Two cardboard paper towel tubes
Scissors
Ruler
Colored adhesive plastic
Marker
Decorative stickers
Thick rug yarn
Ribbon or premade bow
Clear tape

Adult Preparation
1. Cover two paper towel tubes with colored adhesive plastic.
2. Measure and cut the paper towel tubes into 2" wide sections to make small tubes.

Instructions
1. Insert a piece of rug yarn through all the cardboard tubes.
2. With an adult's help, pull and tie the ends of the yarn together with the threaded tubes on it to make a wreath shape. Tape the cardboard tubes together in the back to keep them from wiggling around too much.
3. Decorate the tubes with stickers. Write on them a message or Bible verse, such as "Offer hospitality to one another." 1 Peter 4:9a
4. Tape a bow to the top of the wreath as shown.
5. Hang this wreath on the front door of your home or classroom as a welcome wreath to greet visitors.

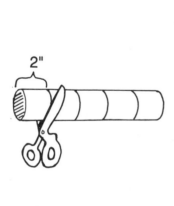

SS3826

Country-Style Miniature Wreath

Materials
Colored tagboard
Pencil
Ruler
Measuring compass
Scissors or hobby knife
Craft glue
Decorative trims (dimensional paint in squeeze bottles, tiny wooden house decorations, wooden heart)
Ribbon

Adult Preparation
1. Draw a round wreath shape, approximately 4" in diameter, on tagboard. Use a measuring compass or trace around a cup and saucer.
2. Use sharp scissors or a hobby knife to cut out the wreath shape.

Instructions
1. Use dimensional squeeze paint to decorate the wreath with this message, "Bless this home!" Write the words directly on the wreath or on little wooden houses which you glue to the wreath.
2. Decorate the wreath with other trims such as a little bow and a wooden heart as shown.
3. Attach a piece of ribbon to the back of the wreath to hang it on the wall.

Other Ideas
1. Cut the wreath shape from a plastic margarine tub lid to be covered with fabric ribbon. (Wrapping the wreath with ribbon will take extra time.)
2. Wrap narrow fabric ribbon around the wreath as shown. Allow extra time to do this unless an adult does it ahead of time.
3. Cut little houses out of colored tagboard. Plan extra time to do this unless an adult does it ahead of time.
4. Use markers to write on the tagboard.

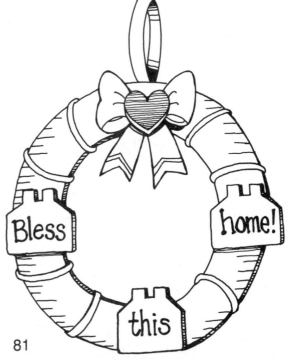

Miniature Chalkboard Ornament

Materials
Miniature framed slate chalkboard ornament (available at craft stores)
White "puff" dimensional paint in squeeze bottle

Instructions
1. Paint words or draw symbols for an inspirational message or a Bible verse on the little chalkboard, such as an "equation" representing God's love: Jesus + Me = LOVE!
2. Let the paint dry before hanging it up.

Other Ideas
1. If you're using "puff" paint, some types puff up after drying in the air. Others require heat to make the paint puff out.
2. Purchase decorative trims and glue them along the frame. Prepainted tiny wooden hearts or red apples glued to the four corners of the frame add a decorative appearance as shown.

SS3826

Wooden Picture Frame

Materials
Four jumbo-size wooden crafts sticks (or tongue depressors)
Craft glue
Scissors
Construction paper
Dimensional paint (in squeeze bottles) or permanent markers
Clear tape
Photograph of your family
Yarn or narrow ribbon

Instructions
1. Glue four large wooden craft sticks together to make a square frame. (Overlap the corners of the sticks as shown.) Hold the sticks in place as they begin to dry.
2. Cut out a square piece of construction paper to fit behind the frame.
3. Glue the construction paper behind the frame.
4. Use dimensional paint or markers to write "Lord, bless our home!" on the frame.
5. Let the paint and glue dry for a few minutes. Put a dab of glue or several bits of rolled tape on the back of a photo. Attach the photo to the center of the construction paper.
6. Tape a bit of yarn or ribbon to the back of the frame to hang it up.

Other Idea
1. Add decorative trims, such as prepainted wooden hearts or tiny wooden houses, to the four corners of the frame.

SS3826

House-Shaped Bible Verse Frame

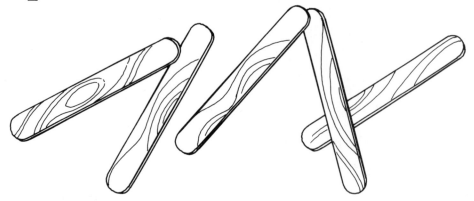

Materials
Five wooden craft sticks
Craft glue
Scissors
Construction paper
Fine-line markers or crayons
Hole punch
Narrow ribbon or yarn

Instructions
1. Glue the craft sticks together in a simple house shape with a slanted roof. Overlap the sticks as shown.
2. Cut a piece of construction paper to fit behind the house.
3. Glue paper to the back of the house frame.
4. Let the glue dry slightly, then write on the construction paper, "But as for me and my household, we will serve the Lord." Joshua 24:15c. Draw flowers below the verse.
5. Punch a hole in the construction paper near the top of the roof.
6. Insert yarn or ribbon through the hole and tie it in a bow.
7. Hang the frame on a wall, door, or bulletin board.

"But as for me and my household, we will serve the Lord."

JOSHUA 24:15c

SS3826

Lace Doily Wall Decoration

Materials

Small wooden embroidery hoop
Round paper or fabric lace doily (several inches larger than the embroidery hoop)
Narrow fabric ribbon
Scissors
Craft glue
Fine-line marker or dimensional paint (in squeeze bottle)

Instructions

1. With an adult's help, separate the two pieces of the embroidery hoop to open it.
2. Place the doily over the smaller inner ring, then snap the larger outer ring over it. (Be careful not to rip the paper doily.) There should be a lacy ruffle around the outside of the hoop.
3. Glue ribbon around the outside edge of the hoop. Make a bow from the ribbon and glue it to the top of the hoop as shown.
4. Use a marker or dimensional paint to write on the center of the doily, "Friends are a blessing!"
5. Give this gift to a friend who is a special blessing in your life. Your friend can hang it as a reminder of your friendship.

Other Idea

1. Turn the hoop, with the lace doily snapped between it, upside down. Cut two round pieces of construction paper the same size as the hoop. Glue one of the paper circles on the back of the doily to cover any holes in the lace. Pour a bit of sweet smelling potpourri mixture in the center area, then glue the other paper circle behind the hoop to keep the potpourri in place. To hang the sachet, tape a loop of ribbon to the back of the hoop.

SS3826

Square Envelope

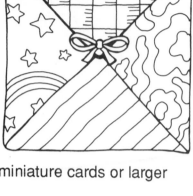

Materials

Heavy wrapping paper, construction paper, or square paper lace doily
Ruler
Pencil
Scissors
Decorative trims (glitter, tiny bows, stickers, etc.)
Craft glue
Clear tape
Markers

Instructions

1. Use a ruler and pencil to draw a square. (Make tiny envelopes for miniature cards or larger envelopes.) Cut out the square.
2. Fold three of the four corners in toward the center of the square as shown. If you're using gift wrap with a printed design on it, the design should be on the outside of the envelope. The three corners should meet in the center.
3. Tape along the edges where the three sides meet.
4. Add trims such as stickers or glue on some glitter or a tiny bow to the outside of the envelope.
5. Make a paper card or a note to fit inside the envelope. (The card could be a heart shape for Valentine's Day.) Write a message or Bible verse on the card. On the outside of the envelope write the name of the person who will receive this card.
6. Fold down the remaining upper flap and tape the envelope shut with the card inside.

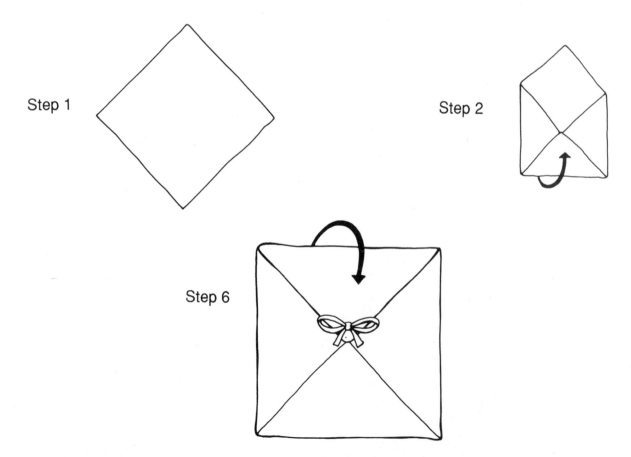

Step 1

Step 2

Step 6

Lace Doily Miniature Basket

Materials
Small paper lace doilies (round, heart-shaped, etc.)
Glue or tape
Decorative trims (glitter, narrow ribbon, chenille stems, etc.)
Paper scraps
Scissors
Decorative stickers
Items to fill basket (notes, tiny dried flowers, candy, etc.)

Instructions
1. Choose the type of basket you wish to make.
2. To make a cone-shaped basket, roll a round doily into a cone and tape the overlapping edges. To make a pocket basket, tape a smaller doily (such as a heart shape) to a larger one, leaving the top edge untaped to form a pocket, or tape two doilies of the same size together along the sides, leaving the top edge untaped.
3. To make a handle, tape a ribbon or chenille stem to the top of your basket.
4. Decorate your basket with stickers, glitter, tiny bows, etc.
5. Fill the basket with a note with a Bible verse on it, candy, dried flowers, etc.
6. Give the basket to someone for a special day such as Mother's Day or Valentine's Day, or hang it on someone's doorknob on May Day.

Other Idea
1. Use fabric doilies which have been soaked in fabric stiffener to make baskets. This will take longer because of the drying time required, and you will need an adult's supervision.

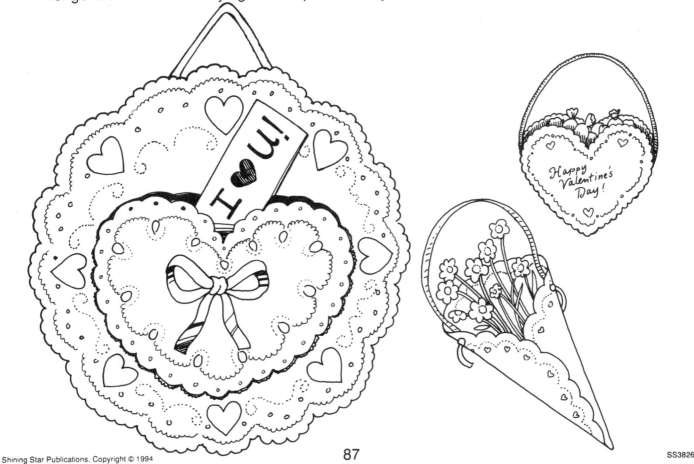

SS3826

Paper Plate Basket

Materials

Two paper plates
Scissors
Stapler and staples
Hole punch
Yarn, ribbon, or chenille stem
Markers
Decorative trims (stickers, glitter glue, etc.)
Clear tape
Items to fill basket (real or artificial flowers, candies, notepad and pencil, etc.)

Instructions

1. Cut paper plates to the shapes shown. The shapes may be the same size, or the front can be smaller than the back piece. Keep the plates rounded or cut them into heart shapes.
2. Staple the two plates together to make a pocket.
3. On the front of the pocket, write a Bible verse or a message such as "Love one another."
4. Decorate the basket with stickers, glitter, etc.
5. Cut a rounded handle from the paper plate itself, attach a chenille stem or ribbon for a handle, or punch a hole in the top of the back side of the project and tie ribbon through the hole to hang the basket.
6. Fill the basket with a memo pad and pencil, candy, or pretty flowers to give as a gift.

Burlap Place Mat

Materials
18" x 12" rectangle of burlap
Sewing machine or nonfray liquid (available at fabric stores)
Scissors
Fabric paint (in squeeze bottles) or permanent markers

Adult Preparation
1. Cut burlap 18" x 12".
2. If possible, hem the edges on a sewing machine or apply nonfray liquid to the fabric edges. Let the fabric dry overnight.
3. You may prefer to leave the edges unhemmed.

Instructions
1. If the burlap edges are not hemmed, pull out some of the threads to make fringed edges.
2. Use fabric paint or markers to decorate your place mat. You may wish to write on it part of a mealtime prayer, such as "God is great! God is good!"
3. Let the paint dry thoroughly before using the place mat.

Other Ideas
1. Place a sheet of scrap paper or newspaper under the burlap so the ink or paint doesn't leak through onto the table.
2. If you have time, make or purchase cut sponge designs or stencils to use with fabric paint. Make country-style designs, such as cats and hearts, on the place mat.
3. Cut decorations from felt and glue them to the mat.
4. If you have extra time, embroider the mat. Mats may also be made from felt or colored construction paper. Cover the construction paper with clear adhesive plastic to protect it.
5. If you have time, make a place mat for each member of your family.
6. Make mats to hang on the wall. Attach a stick or dowel and tie yarn to the stick to hang up the mat.

 SS3826

Food Puppets

Materials

Round or oval fruits and vegetables (apples, oranges, potatoes, etc.)
Items to decorate the fruits and vegetables (cloves, raisins, nuts, grapes, cherries, blueberries, strawberries, carrot and celery chunks, lettuce, etc.)
Toothpicks
Narrow wooden dowel or chopstick (approximately 8" long)
Craft glue or low temperature glue gun and glue sticks
Fabric scraps

Instructions

1. With an adult's help, push a wooden chopstick or a dowel into the bottom of a fruit or vegetable to make the head and neck of the puppet.
2. The stick will also be the handle for the puppet. Hold onto the handle while you decorate the puppet head as a character from a Bible story.
3. Using toothpicks, stick raisins, cloves, and berries into the puppet's head for eyes, nose, mouth, and ears. Lettuce works well for hair and beards, though it wilts fairly quickly.
4. If you don't plan to eat the food later, you may glue on some items. Use a glue gun with an adult's help. You may need to hold some items in place while they dry, which will take extra time.
5. Use fabric scraps to make a Bible-time head covering for the puppet.
6. Use the puppet to act out a Bible story. If your friends make puppets too, work together to plan a puppet play to share with others.

Fabric scraps
Raisin
Cherry half
Carrot piece
Lettuce
Lettuce
Chopstick

Carrot curls
Cherry halves
Grape half
Cloves
Potato
Carrot curls

SS3826

Food Faces

Materials
Paper plate
Marker
Plastic knife or spatula
Flat, round food item (large cookie, rice cake, cracker, or circle cut from bread)
Coating to represent "skin" coloring (cream cheese, peanut butter, frosting)
Small food items (raisins, tiny candies, berries, cherry tomatoes, carrot pieces, celery pieces, nuts, etc.)
Lettuce or alfalfa sprouts
Toothpicks

Instructions
1. Along the outside edge of the paper plate, use the marker to write "Jesus loves me!" You may wish to use your name or the name of a friend in place of the word *me*, to personalize this project.
2. Put the flat, round food item in the center of the plate. (Make sure it isn't over the words.)
3. With an adult's help, use a knife or spatula to spread the coating over the round food item. Choose a color of coating that looks like your own skin if you want the face to look like you.
4. Use small food items to decorate the project. Push the items directly into the coating or use toothpicks to stick them on. Leafy lettuce or alfalfa sprouts work well for hair.
5. Display your project for awhile or give it to someone. You or someone else can enjoy eating it later!

Other Idea
1. Make a fun display for a classroom, with a number of children and teacher(s) making these treats. The display will remind everyone that we were all created to look different and unique, and Jesus loves each of us just as we are. Have a party and enjoy eating your treats!

                                   SS3826

Candy Treats

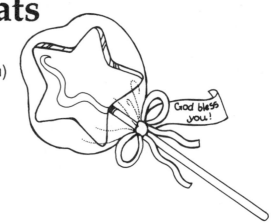

Materials
Candy (see tips on page 93 if you want to make your own)
Colored or clear plastic wrap or cellophane
Narrow curling ribbon
Hole punch
Scissors
Scraps of paper
Fine-line markers

Adult Preparation
1. If you want to make your own candy, use your own favorite recipes or buy large candy chips which can be heated and poured into mold shapes. (You can purchase these materials at a hobby shop.)
2. Purchase candy, such as lollipops.

Instructions
1. Decide how you want to wrap your candy to make a gift package. For example, you can make several lollipops into a bouquet.
2. Wrap the candy in plastic wrap or cellophane. With an adult's help, tie it in a bundle or a bouquet. Use cute candy shapes, such as flowers, butterflies, stars, hearts, lambs, or teddy bears, to share a message of God's love on special days, such as Easter, Christmas, or Valentine's Day.
3. If you're using curling ribbon, ask an adult to help you use scissors to make it curl.
4. Make a little gift tag from paper. Write on it a message such as "God bless you!" Punch a hole to attach the tag to the ribbon on the candy gift.

Other Ideas
1. Deliver a bouquet of candy treats with a card to someone who is sick, sad, or lonely.
2. Use animal molds to make animals from the creation story in Genesis or make animal pairs from the Noah's ark story.

Candy-Making Tips

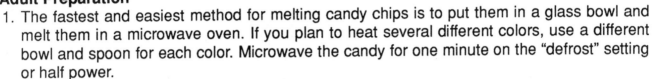

Materials

Plastic candy molds
Candy melting chips (in a variety of colors)
Microwave oven
Microwaveable glass bowls
Wooden or plastic spoons
Refrigerator
Cotton dish towel

Adult Preparation

1. The fastest and easiest method for melting candy chips is to put them in a glass bowl and melt them in a microwave oven. If you plan to heat several different colors, use a different bowl and spoon for each color. Microwave the candy for one minute on the "defrost" setting or half power.
2. Stir the candy, then microwave it for another minute.
3. Continue microwaving in thirty-second intervals, stirring after each interval, until the candy is completely melted and is smooth and creamy.
4. Pour the melted candy into the mold immediately. It will begin to harden as it cools, so make sure the child is ready to participate as soon as the candy is melted.

Instructions

1. With an adult's help, pour or spoon candy into the mold to fill the shapes.
2. Lightly tap the filled mold several times on a counter to make sure there are no air bubbles. If the mold is made from clear plastic, look underneath it. Tap gently where you see any air bubbles.

Adult Follow-Up

1. Put the mold in the refrigerator to cool. Small candies will harden in approximately thirty minutes.
2. Once the underside of the mold looks frosted, without dark spots, the candy is ready to be removed from the mold.
3. Turn the mold upside down over a dish towel.
4. Let the child help you tap the mold or bend it slightly to release the candy.
5. Break any excess edges off the candy.

Other Ideas

1. Check often as you melt the candy chips to keep them from burning. Precool the candy mold by putting it in the refrigerator while you melt the candy.
2. You may prefer to melt the candy in a double boiler or an electric skillet.
3. Make sure candy molds and utensils are totally dry before using them. Water spots will make streaks in the candy as it hardens.
4. Make hard candies and lollipops by using hard-candy recipes and special molds. Sticks and molds for lollipops may be purchased at hobby shops.
5. Use these ideas to make gift projects such as those described on page 92.

SS3826

Bible Theme Cinnamon Ornaments

Materials
Cinnamon clay (see page 95 for recipe, ingredients, and tools needed)
White flour
Rolling pin and flat surface, such as wooden cutting board or table
Cookie cutters (plastic or metal Bible-related shapes: heart, lamb, cross, star, etc.; and alphabet letters)
Sharpened pencil or plastic straw
Narrow ribbon
Scissors

Adult Instructions
1. Prepare a batch of cinnamon clay by following the directions on page 95.
2. Prepare a flat work surface by dusting it lightly with flour or cinnamon.

Instructions
1. With an adult's help, use a rolling pin to flatten a portion of clay to $1/4$" thickness.
2. Use cookie cutters to make clay ornaments in shapes that remind you of Bible stories or themes. Use alphabet letter shapes to spell words such as "Love" or "Joy," or use the sharpened end of a pencil to engrave words in the clay ornaments.
3. Make holes with the pencil or a plastic straw to hang the ornaments later.

Adult Follow-Up
1. Bake the clay ornaments or let them dry according to the directions on page 95.
2. After the ornaments are dry, tie ribbons through the holes to hang them.

Other Ideas
1. The ornaments will shrink slightly as they dry.
2. Use glitter glue or dimensional paints (in squeeze bottles) to decorate the ornaments after they are dried or cooled.

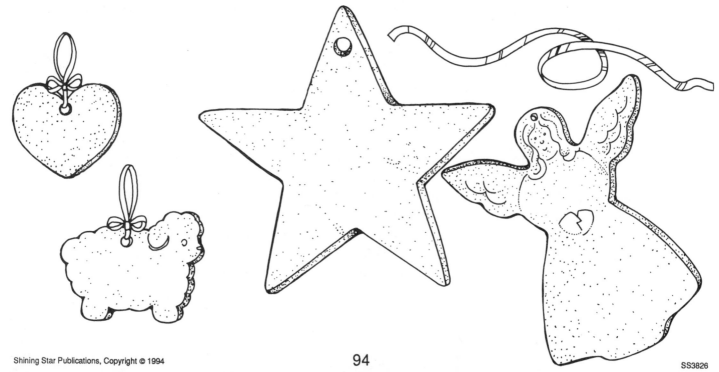

SS3826

Cinnamon Clay

Ingredients
1 cup of ground cinnamon
4 tablespoons of white glue
$3/4$ to 1 cup of water

Tools and Other Equipment
Mixing bowl
Large spoon
Refrigerator
Waxed paper or a cookie sheet
(with oven and pot holder)

Adult Preparation
1. Stir together cinnamon, glue, and water. Keep stirring until the mixture is the consistency of cookie dough.
2. Put the clay in the refrigerator for two hours until thoroughly chilled. Remove it from the refrigerator and knead it. You can do this in advance or help the child do it.

Instructions
1. Sprinkle some cinnamon on your work surface. Put the chilled clay on the sprinkled surface. Ask an adult to show you how to knead the clay. Use your fingers and the palms of your hands to knead the clay until it is smooth and not too sticky.
2. Sprinkle more cinnamon on the surface as you continue to work.
3. Roll and shape the clay to make three-dimensional objects, such as animals for Noah's ark or brick-like water wells and figures for other Bible-time scenes. Simply roll the clay into coils and mold other shapes as you would use any other type of clay.

Adult Follow-Up
1. Put the shapes on waxed paper to dry them at room temperature. Drying will take at least four days.
2. To dry the figures more quickly, bake them on a cookie sheet in a warm oven for two hours.

Other Ideas
1. Substitute some of the glue with applesauce. This will enhance the sweet smell. Remember, the clay is not meant to be eaten since it has glue in it.
2. Store the clay in a refrigerator if not using it immediately after preparing it. Let the clay become room temperature before using it.
3. To make flat ornaments, sprinkle some cinnamon on a flat surface and use a rolling pin to roll out the clay until it's $1/4$" thick. Follow the directions on page 94 to cut out Bible theme shapes using cookie cutters. Flat ornaments take approximately four days to dry at room temperature. They should be turned over with a spatula twice a day while drying so the edges don't curl. To dry them more quickly, heat them on a cookie sheet in an oven.
4. This amount of clay will make six large ornaments or other similarly sized projects. The number will vary depending on the sizes and shapes of the projects.

 SS3826

"Son"shine Award!

Presented to:

for

COOL WORK!

"Jesus is my "Son"shine!

Stay Cool in the "Son"!

SS3826